The Supernatural Ways of God

The Supernatural Ways of God

REVEALING THE WAY OF THE LORD

Duncan Katende Ndugwa

Foreword by Rev. Dr. Solomon M. Mwalili

RESOURCE *Publications* · Eugene, Oregon

THE SUPERNATURAL WAYS OF GOD
Revealing the Way of the Lord

Copyright © 2022 Duncan Katende Ndugwa. All rights reserved. Except for brief quotations in critical publications or reviews, no part of this book may be reproduced in any manner without prior written permission from the publisher. Write: Permissions, Wipf and Stock Publishers, 199 W. 8th Ave., Suite 3, Eugene, OR 97401.

Resource Publications
An Imprint of Wipf and Stock Publishers
199 W. 8th Ave., Suite 3
Eugene, OR 97401

www.wipfandstock.com

PAPERBACK ISBN: 978-1-6667-5571-8
HARDCOVER ISBN: 978-1-6667-5572-5
EBOOK ISBN: 978-1-6667-5573-2

All rights reserved. No portion of this book may be reproduced in any form, stored in retrieval system, or transmitted in any form or by any means-electronic, mechanical, photocopy, recording, scanning, other-except for brief quotations in critical reviews or articles, without the prior written permission of the publisher, except as provided by the United States of America copyright law.

Unless otherwise noted, Scripture taken from the New King James Version®. Copyright © 1982 by Thomas Nelson. Used by permission. All rights reserved.

Scripture quotations marked CJB are taken from the Complete Jewish Bible by David H. Stern. Copyright © 1998. All rights reserved. Used by permission of Messianic Jewish Publishers, 6120 Day Long Lane, Clarksville, MD 21029. www.messianicjewish.net.

Scripture quotations marked (NLT) are taken from the Holy Bible, New Living translation, copyright ©1996, 2004, 2015 by Tyndale House Foundation. Used by permission of Tyndale House Publishers, Carol Stream, Illinois 60188. All rights reserved.

All Scripture Hebrew and Greek words and definitions of those words are taken from from the NEW AMERICAN STANDARD EXHAUSTIVE CONCORDANCE.®, © Copyright 1981 by The Lockman Foundation. Used by permission. (www.Lockman.org)

All Hebrew root words and definitions were quoted from Pealim.com (https://www.pealim.com/constructor/) with written permission.

All bold, italics, underlined words in Scripture quotations, or words with quotation marks and parenthesis in paragraphs were added by the author for emphasis.

While the author had made every effort to provide accurate internet addresses at the time of publication, neither the publisher nor the author assumes any responsibility for errors or changes that occur after publication.

Any internet addresses, phone numbers, or company or product information printed in this book are offered as a resource and are not intended in any way to be or to imply an endorsement by the publisher and /or author, not does the publisher and/or author vouch for the existence, content, or service of these sites, phone numbers, companies, or products beyond the life of this book.

Contents

Foreword ix

Chapter 1: Introduction ix
  The Heavenly Classroom ix
  The Bubbling Up x
  Wisdom in Simplicity x
  Why the Hebrew? xi

Chapter 2: Revealing the Way of the LORD (Derek Yahweh) 1
  The Revelation of Walking with God 1
  Guarding the Way 4
  Abraham the Keeper of the Way of the LORD 5
  Abraham the Guardian and the New Testament Connection 7
  Jeremiah's Great and Foolish Men 9
  Making Straight the Way of the LORD 10
  "Tevilah Teshuva": Preparing the Way and Making It Straight 14
  The Abram the Hebrew and John the Immerser 15
  John's Tevilah Teshuva and the Will of God 19
  Immersion of Repentance and Fulfillment of All Righteousness 21
  John's Immersion and the Kingdom of God 22
  Yeshua, the Revealer of the Way of the LORD 23

Chapter 3: The Blessing For All the Families on the Earth 28
  The Convergence of the Gospel 28
  The Law of Faith and the Law of Righteousness 30
  God's Will: *His Way of Righteousness* 33
  God's Way of Righteousness is the Judgement of God 40
  The Fairness of the Way of the Lord in question 42
  Unveiling the Word Righteousness 42
  The Circles of Righteousness 46

The Predicament of Right Standing with God 49
Unveiling the Blessing of Abraham 51

Chapter 4: The Adam Principle 56
    Adam, The Two voices & the Two Trees 56
    The Adam Blueprint 60
    Adam, the Glory of God 63
    Defining Adam 63
    The Revelation of Mashiach and the Son of Man 66
    God's Spectacular Reconciliation Through the Last Adam 71
    Out Of His Side, You Came Forth 75
    Understanding Being Born Again 78

Chapter 5: The Trees in the Garden 84
    Tree of Life Versus Tree of Knowledge 84
    The Separation of Light and Darkness 88
    Adam's Eyes Being Opened 93
    Becoming like God knowing Good and Evil? 95
    Parable of the Fig Tree 97
    The Covering of Fig Leaves 103
    The Light from The Tree of Knowledge of Good and Evil 104

Chapter 6: From Filthy Rags To Glorious Garments 106
    Moshe's Law of Righteousness 106
    The Spiritual Nature of Self-Righteousness 108
    The Way of the Lord: Fully Revealed and fully Manifest 111
    Walking from Faith to Faith 112

Chapter 7: The Prophet Like Moses 123
    The Prophet from The Region of The Galilee 123
    The Zohar, The Star and The Scepter 129

Chapter 8: A Gift from Heaven 132
    Righteousness Looks Down from Heaven 132
    Imputed Sin 134
    Imputed Righteousness: The Joy of Forgiveness 139
    A Deeper Understanding Of Righteousness (Tzedakah) 139

About the Author 145
Bibliography 147

Foreword

When God created man, He desired to keep a close fellowship with him, and in deed this was so until the fall of man. As long as Adam and his wife, Eve, observed the directives of God, all was well. But the moment the Serpent found his way into their lives through lies about the tree of the knowledge of good and evil, this fellowship was destroyed.

However, God in His Love had to come up with a way of restoring this relationship with man, through the promise of a Savior. This promise was not fulfilled immediately. Through generations, God continued to call man to walk in His ways, but because of the sin of Adam, man has not fully walked in the ways of God.

Scripture gives us examples of people who understood the ways of God and walked with Him. They include Enock, Noah, Abraham, and Elijah among others. They heard the voice of God and obeyed. Hebrews chapter twelve verse one tells us how God in the past spoke to our fathers through the prophets at many times and in different ways. Some of these ways included dreams, like in the case of Jacob (Genesis 28:12–15); Fire like in the case of Moses (Exodus 3:1–10) and bright light like in the conversion of Saul of Tarsus (Acts 9:1–6).

Through all these different means, God would make His ways known to man. In order to understand the ways of God, man needs to have a deep relationship with God, for the things of God are not known to man unless they are revealed by His Spirit (1 Corinthians 2:10–11).

In this book, Duncan Ndugwa has gone into great depths to open the eyes of our understanding concerning the ways of God. He begins by sharing his experience of the night dream in which he saw the heavenly classroom and the huge magnificent looking book which read in bold, HIS WAYS. From this experience, he goes ahead to glean through Scripture to inform us of God's plan for mankind right from creation to the fall, and

Foreword

God's subsequent plan for salvation through the second Adam (God's Son Jesus Christ). So, as you read through this great book, you will be thoroughly informed of the ways of God and how to walk in them.

Rev. Dr. Solomon M. Mwalili, D. Min.
Senior Pastor, Free Pentecostal Fellowship in Kenya
Embakasi Church, Nairobi.

Chapter 1

Introduction

The Heavenly Classroom

The journey to authoring this book began with a night dream. It was a short dream in which I was in a classroom at a small desk. Somehow, I was the only student, but I knew this was a classroom in another dimension i.e., in Heaven. A huge magnificent-looking Book covered in Purple Velvet was handed to me to read. It had *Gold* inscriptions on the front, which read in bold: *"His Ways."* When I opened the Book, all I saw was white bright *Light* shining from the pages into my face and then I woke up. I knew from that point the knowledge of the ways of God was imprinted on my heart by the light that shone from the pages of the Book.

The bible says "the God of our Lord Jesus the Messiah, the glorious Father, to give you a spirit of wisdom and revelation, so that you will have full knowledge of him. I pray that *he will give light to the eyes of your hearts*, so that you will understand the hope to which he has called you, what rich glories there are in the inheritance he has promised his people" (Ephesians 1:17–18 CJB).

God gave *"...light to the eyes..."* of my heart. In God's light, there is knowledge, which is *"...the light of the knowledge...."* "For it is the God who commanded light to shine out of darkness, who *has shone in our hearts* to give *the light of the knowledge* of the glory of God in the face of Jesus Christ." (2 Corinthians 4:6) I expected that Knowledge now in my heart to soon *'bubble up'* or enlighten my mind. It took another three years for my mind to finally grasp what I could perceive.

Introduction

The Bubbling Up

It was a Saturday night in Salina, Kansas. As I laid on a comfortable bed in the spare bedroom of Pastor Larry and Ethel Knox's house; preparing for my sermon the next day at their church, Word of Faith Church, when it all happened. My mind was filled to what felt like the brim with Light! Suddenly, I could see it all and I knew from then on, I would never preach the same messages I had previously been preaching.

My message had to radically change as I saw how, like a Master Artist's signature that identifies the Artist and makes the artwork unique and valuable, the ways of God are spread out like a unique golden thread in a handwoven tapestry that stretches from the Beginning in the Book of Genesis all through to the end of the New Testament. However, as I was drafting this book, I realized that I had found favor in the Eyes of God to be shown his ways, to walk in them. I give Glory to God for everything you will read in this book as I know I could not have produced any of it. The Holy Spirit is truly the Best Teacher!!

Wisdom in simplicity

I know, it sounds too easy to receive all this, right? Well, I figured out one thing in this journey: though God is full of unimaginable glorious complexity, derived from his glorious wisdom, He chose to make things *simple to understand* for those *who believe*. He does this by *"revealing"* those things that He has purposely hidden for those who believe in Him. Those who do not believe display their wisdom as anything that is outstandingly *complex*.

Their continuous efforts to figure out the complexity of God in their own wisdom snares them, which results in them knowing Him *less*, as it says, "for since, in the wisdom of God, *the world through (its) wisdom did not know God*, it pleased God through the foolishness of the message preached to save those *who believe.*" (1 Corinthians 1:21)

God's message to those who believe is made simple because they rely on Him, not on themselves *(with child-like or humble hearts)*. He teaches them his Wisdom: "These things we also speak, *not in words which man's wisdom teaches* but *which the Holy Spirit teaches,* comparing spiritual things with spiritual. But *the natural man* does not receive the things of the Spirit of God, for *they are foolishness to him*; nor can he know them, because they are spiritually discerned." (1 Corinthians 2:13–14)

Introduction

But to those who do not believe, the simple message seems foolish in their eyes. So, since the natural man's wisdom is rooted in complexity, when they attempt to understand God on their own, they will find deeper complexity, which is a veil. That is why an unbeliever cannot understand when they read the Bible: there is a veil on their eyes. The veil is their natural wisdom, which seems so complex but *is coming to nothing*.

First Corinthians 2:6–7 says, "However, we speak wisdom among those who are mature, yet not the wisdom of this age, nor of the rulers of this age, who are coming to nothing. But we speak the wisdom of God in a mystery, the hidden wisdom which God ordained before the ages for our glory." As it says above, "*...we speak the wisdom of God in a mystery....*" It also says, "*...the hidden wisdom which God ordained....*"

This wisdom of God is a mystery, and it is hidden; it is concealed according to Proverbs 25:2, "It is the glory of God *to conceal a matter,* But the glory of kings is *to search out a matter.*" The wisdom of God is concealed from who? It is concealed or hidden from those who do not believe! But for those who believe, they can search it out because it is no longer concealed. So, for the believer, the corruption starts when we treat spiritual things, which are taught by God as though they are not complex enough. Some believers look for complexity and become corrupted. In the New Testament, Paul cautions the Corinthians from having their minds corrupted by complexity: "But I fear, lest somehow, *as the serpent deceived Eve by his craftiness*, so your *minds may be corrupted* from the *simplicity* that is in Christ." (2 Corinthians 11:3)

This revelation graciously given to me by God in this book is only *one* of his ways (more books to come), which is *simple*, but it is what I call the main ingredient for the most powerful message in the Universe: *The Good News i.e., the Gospel of Mashiach!* As such, in the following passages, do not be tempted to look for hyper-worldly or natural complexities. Rather, as the book unfolds like a scroll, see the *simplicity* of his ways, discover his grace, and know him.

Why the Hebrew?

In 2005, I had an encounter with the Lord after expressing my frustration with not understanding the Bible. My complaint was, *"All I want is the truth!."* Then He answered me by saying, *"Are you ready for the truth?"* I said, *"Yes!"* Then He said, *"Get ready because I Am going to turn everything you know upside down!*" And boy was He right. To turn something upside down is to *flip it* or *turn it over!* "For then *I will restore* to the peoples *a pure language,* that they may call on the Name of the LORD, to serve Him with one accord." (Zephaniah 3:9)

The phrase "*...I will restore...*" is translated from the Hebrew word "*ehpoch*" (אֶהְפֹּךְ), which means, "*I will turn over.*" The Lord has such high wisdom, his normal speech sounds like *riddles* to us. However, He does reveal the hidden things to you. He does unveil his mysteries. As you can see, He was telling me the truth I was looking for was in what the Bible calls "*Yehudit*" (יְהוּדִית), which means "*Jewish*" or what is normally referred to as the Hebrew language and culture! Why? This is the language and culture He gave the Hebrews. He is the "*...God of the Hebrews...*" (*Exodus 3:18*) after all. It was Him Who gave the Hebrews their language and the culture. What about us?

God gave us different languages, as noted by the Torah concerning Noah's three sons (*Japheth, Ham, and Shem*) from whom all humanity came from after the flood: "The *sons of Japheth* were... From these the coastland peoples of the Gentiles were separated into their lands, *everyone according to his language*, according to their families, into their nations." (Genesis 10:2–5) "These were the *sons of Ham*, according to their families, *according to their languages*, in their lands and in their nations." (Genesis 10:20) "These were the *sons of Shem*, according to their families, *according to their languages*, in their lands according to their nations." (Genesis 10:31)

There were different languages on the Earth after the flood. However, just like we have English today as a language commonly spoken around the world, the whole earth at the time of the sons of Noah also had one *common* language and speech as well: "Now the whole earth had *one language* and *one speech.*" (Genesis 11:1) Since the people all wanted to ascend to Heaven to make a Name for themselves, God confused their language, which caused them to scatter over the face of the earth. What is interesting is that right before this *scattering*, the Torah mentioned the genealogies of all three sons: "*The sons of Japheth were Gomer, Magog, Madai, Javan, Tubal, Meshech, and Tiras.*" (Genesis 10:2) "*The sons of Ham were Cush, Mizraim, Put, and Canaan.*" (Genesis 10:6) "*The sons of Shem were Elam, Asshur, Arphaxad, Lud, and Aram.*" (Genesis 10:22)

Right after the great scattering, only Shem's genealogy was mentioned from the book of Genesis 11:10 "*This is the genealogy of Shem...*" This was a hint to show where God was going and which line, He stayed with and

Introduction

would entrust with his language and culture. In Genesis, we are introduced to Abram (a descendant of Shem), as a *"Hebrew."* "Then one who had escaped came and told *Abram the Hebrew*, for he dwelt by the terebinth trees." (Genesis 14:13)

The English word *"Hebrew"* in the above passage is translated from the Hebrew word *"Ivri"* (עִבְרִי). Abram was the first to be called by God a *Hebrew (Ivri)* and the language the Hebrews spoke was called *"Yehudit"*: "But Then Eliakim, Shebna, and Joah said to the Rabshakeh, "Please speak to your servants in Aramaic, for we understand it; and *do not speak to us in Hebrew* in the hearing of the people who are on the wall." (Isaiah 36:11)

The word *"Hebrew"* in the above verse is translated from the Hebrew word *"Yehudit"* (יְהוּדִית), which we call *"Jewish."* However, in such Books as Nehemiah (5:1) for example, and in modern terms, the terms are reversed where we refer to the people as *Jewish* and the language as *Hebrew*! Abram was a Hebrew who spoke Jewish! Abram's descendants are Jewish and speak Hebrew. These may be interchangeable. Regardless, this is the language that is described in *Zephaniah 3:9* as a *"...pure language...".*

I heard *"Aramaic"* many times referred to as a part of the Jewish culture, however, in the previous verse (*Isaiah 36:11*), the word *"Aramaic"* is translated from the Hebrew word, *"Aramit"* (אֲרָמִית), which the Strong's Concordance calls, *"...the language of Aram (Syria)..."* The passage mentions *"Rabshkeh"* who was sent by *"...Sennacherib King of Assyria..."* (*Isaiah 36:1*). I do not believe Aramaic was the language God gave the Hebrews. It seems Abram and his descendants were able to *understand and speak* Aramaic because he was from *"...Ur of the Chaldeans..."* (*Genesis 11:31*), as the Chaldeans also spoke Aramaic: "Then *the Chaldeans spoke to the king in Aramaic*, "O king, live forever! Tell your servants the dream, and we will give the interpretation." (Daniel 2:4)

Not that I have researched or studied this in-depth but what the verses above show, I do not yet see an intertwining between Hebrew and Aramaic but due to the closeness of the people at different periods in history, it was easy for the Hebrews to speak and understand Aramaic.

The Lord made it clear to me that the Truth I was searching for, He encoded within the Hebrew language and culture. Besides the Lord Whom I serve, *Yeshua My Mashiach is Jewish!* So, I was listening to the *God of the Hebrews* teaching me about his ways encoded or hidden within his culture. "All Scripture is given by inspiration of God, and is profitable for doctrine, for reproof, for correction, for instruction in righteousness, …." (2 Timothy 3:16)

To make a point, it just so happened that most of all the men and women who were inspired to author the Books of the Bible, we love were Jewish. Therefore, in this book as we discover the ways of God, I will use a lot of Hebrew words to unlock the treasures hidden in the mysteries of God.

Chapter 2

Revealing the Way of the LORD (Derek YHWH)

The Revelation of Walking with God

According to the Scriptures, a man named Enoch never died but was taken by God: "And *Enoch walked with God*; and he was not, *for God took him.*" (Genesis 5:24) Enoch *walked with God* before being taken by God.

To walk means you must go along a certain predetermined road, way, or path. It was not just aimless walking. If you walk on the road or on the path the Lord walks on, you will walk *with* God because He walks on his own *chosen* ways and paths. Adam and Eve used to walk with God before their fall. Even after eating from the Tree of the knowledge of good and evil, it is evident in the following verse that God had come *to walk* with them, but they hid due to the shame of their sin:

"And they heard the sound of the Lord God *walking* in the garden in the cool of the day, and Adam and his wife hid themselves from the presence of the Lord God among the trees of the garden." (Genesis 3:8) God came walking towards a place where He would meet with them, but they hid. The word *"sound"* in the above verse from the New King James Version is translated from the Hebrew the word *"Qol"* (קוֹל), which is translated many times as a *"Voice."* So, they heard the *"…Voice of the LORD God walking…."*

The King James Version confirms this: "And they heard the *Voice of the Lord God walking* in the garden in the cool of the day: (Genesis 3:8) A voice walking? Yes! The *Voice of the LORD God walking*: is not that amazing! The voice was walking, in the *"Cool of the day."* The word *"Cool"* in English in the above verse was translated from the Hebrew word *"Ruach,"* (רוח), which can be translated as *"Wind"* or *"Spirit."* They used to walk with the voice of the LORD God in the *Spirit* of the day!

This has been my experience with God: there is a path He brings for you to walk on. Whenever it happens with me, I see Him pass by and He always says to me, *"...follow me!"* and when I do, it is a fast-paced ride on a *path* that is already set, and I get to see things along the Way! Let me make it plainer: The *Voice of God* would come to meet with Adam and Eve and then put them on this Spirit or *"Wind"* path on which they would walk together with God!

The wind has *"direction"* meaning it comes from somewhere and goes somewhere and it has the power to propel you into the direction it is going! This wind would propel them forward, moving with the voice of God! The wind is what birds, boats with sails and airplanes use to move! So, there was a wind pathway or *Spirit pathway* called the *Cool of the day (Ruach of the Day)*, that they would walk on together with the voice of the LORD God. This reveals the mystery of the verse when Yeshua says the following: *"The Wind* blows where it wishes, and *you hear the sound of it*, but cannot tell where it comes from and where it goes. *So is everyone who is born of the Spirit."* (John 3:8)

Using the two Hebrew words for wind and sound as noted above, I could also see the above verse the following way: "The *Ruach (Spirit)* blows where it wishes, and you hear *the Voice (sound)* of it but cannot tell where it comes from and where it goes. *So is everyone who is born of the Spirit."* The reason He says you *".... cannot tell where it comes from and where it goes..."* is because you do not lead the Spirit: The Spirit leads you! It says *"...in the Cool of the day...."* So, which day?

There are two types of days noted in Genesis. There is the day, we know as the one made evident by the *illumination of the Sun* on the earth and there is the day that is referenced as *Light*, which was before the creation of the Sun. "Then God said, *"Let there be light;"* and there was light. And God saw the light, that it was good; and God divided the light from the darkness. *God called the Light Day*, and the darkness He called Night. So, the evening and the morning were the first day." (Genesis 1:3–5)

As you can see above, before creating *"anything"* on the earth, God said, *"Let there be Light."* But note that this *"creative"* Light, the Bible says, *"...God called the Light Day..."* So, there is this *Light* called *"Day,"* yet the sun has not been created at this point! Then the sun is created in the following passage but note carefully what it says:

"Then God said, "*Let there be Lights* in the firmament of the heavens *to divide* the day from the night; and let them be for signs and seasons, and for days and years; and let them be for lights in the firmament of the heavens *to give Light on the earth;*" and it was so. *Then God made two great Lights: the greater Light to rule the day,* and the lesser light to rule the night. He made the stars also. God set them in the firmament of the heavens to give light on the earth, and to rule over the day and over the night, and to divide the light from the darkness. And God saw that it was good. So, the evening and the morning were the *fourth day*." (Genesis 1:14-19)

In verse sixteen, it says *"…God made two great Lights…"* i.e. He made *two* additional light(s) from the *Light* that came in verse three. The function of these lights was to give *Light to the Earth!* Well, we know the garden was in the East of Eden, not necessarily on the Earth. But the Bible already notes in verse nineteen, that this was the fourth day! If the Sun was the only day, shouldn't it say in verse nineteen that this was the *First* day?

Let me explain as God defined the *Creative Light* in verse three as *"Day,"* it means He sent out seven blasts of the creative light called *"Day"* to create the Universe in seven creative light days with the Seventh creative blast being the brightest in which He rested, He called Holy, and He blessed! That says something about the Sabbath (that is another book).

So, the *"Cool of the Day"* is not the day connected to the illumination of the Sun, which gives light to the Earth. Remember in Hebrew, the *"Cool of the Day"* reads as the *"Ruach of the Day"* or *"Wind of the Day."* As *Wind* or *Ruach* can be translated as *"Spirit,"* it can be read also as the *"Spirit of the Day."* However, which Day? The *Light* called Day as in Genesis 1:5! As such, the *Cool of the Day* was the *"Spirit of the Light."* Hope that makes sense! Adam and Eve walked with God in his light pathway. The light pathway was named day! They walked in the same *Light* mentioned in Genesis 1:3 and 1:5!

"For with You is the fountain of life; *In Your Light we see Light.*" (Psalm 36:9) You see Light when you enter *His Light*! So, here is an example of this from John: "I was *in the Spirit* on *the Lord's Day*, and I heard behind me *a loud voice,* as of a trumpet," (Revelation 1:10) Notice, he says he was *"…in the Spirit…"* i.e., *"…in the Ruach…"* and *"…on the LORD's Day…,"* i.e., in the *"…Ruach of the day…."* He makes it clear by making sure we do not think this was a natural day from the Sun, but he calls it *the Lord's Day* meaning he was riding on the *Lord's Light*. John was in the wind traveling on the *Light* called the Lord's Day. He was on the Spirit pathway already and then he heard, *"…a loud Voice like trumpet…."* Just like Adam and Eve, you notice three ingredients to John's encounter: *the Voice, the Spirit, and the Day!*

Look at Abraham: "Then the LORD *appeared to him* by the terebinth trees of Mamre, as he was *sitting in the tent door in the heat of the day."* (Genesis 18:1)

Like John, Abraham was *"sitting"* in the tent door in the *"heat of the day."* The Hebrew word for *"door"* is usually *"delet"* (דֶּלֶת), but in the above passage, it is the word, *"Pethach"* (פֶּתַח), which means an *"opening, doorway, entrance."* It is also interesting that the word *"tent"* in the English above is from the Hebrew word *"ohel"* (אֹהֶל), from the root word *"ahal"* (אָהַל), which means *"shine."* So, Abraham was *sitting* at the *entrance of the shining heat of the Day* and the Lord appeared! Why heat? He was not moving! The wind comes to move you and it cools you: Abraham was *"sitting"* in the light, which warms you like a fire!

Simple? It can be. You can walk or talk with God in the *"cool of the day (His Light)"* or in the *"heat of the Day (His Light)"*! "But if *we walk* in the light as He is in the light," (I John 1:7) Be in *His Light*, sit in the warmth of the *Light* and wait for Him or move with his Spirit while being led by his voice: that's Walking with God! So, to walk with God, Adam, Eve, and John above had to walk with his voice in the Spirit *pathway*. This is how Enoch *"…walked with God three hundred years…."* To emphasize, Enoch did this for three hundred years!! No wonder it says, *"…and he was not, for God took him…."* Can we take time in a day to do this?

Guarding the Way

It is also interesting to note that when Adam is thrown out of the garden, we find in the following verse that *cherubim* and a flaming sword are guarding *the Way* to the *Tree of Life*, not the Tree itself! "So, He drove out the man; and He placed cherubim at the east of the garden of Eden, and a flaming sword which turned every way, to guard the Way to the tree of life." (Genesis 3:24)

Adam was denied access to *the Way* to the *Tree of Life*. Imagine you are driving on a highway with exits to other highways, each labeled with a sign. Imagine one of the exit signs says *"Tree of Life"* but it is closed and has guards to make sure no one passes. God has *Ways* and one of them is called the *Way to the Tree of Life*. By grace, Enoch found the Way(s) of God and walked with God on them. As such, he was able to walk with God to a point that *"...he was not, for God took him...."*

That is why Godly men like Moses sought to know the Way(s) of God as noted below, so that they may walk with God as Enoch walked with God. "Now therefore, I pray, If I have found Grace in Your sight, show me now your way, that I may know you and that I may find Grace in your sight...." (Exodus 33:13) Knowing the ways of God and walking on them gives you access to know Him, as Moses mentioned above and much more. Even King David understood this as noted in the following verse: "*Show me Your ways, O LORD; Teach me Your paths*. Lead me in Your truth and teach me, For You are the God of my salvation; On You I wait all day." (Psalm 25:4–5)

The *ways* of God in the above verse are like *superhighways* and the paths are like exits onto country roads to small towns. Once on the superhighway, the lanes are open, fast, and well-lit but the paths can be narrower, slower and can be unlit at night. So, God must show us his ways and teach us his paths.

Moses and David were not asking for mere experiences, they wanted to walk with God as Enoch had walked with God. They were asking to know the ways and paths that righteous men like Enoch and Abraham found to walk with God. The ways and paths of God give you access to significant things in the Kingdom of God and the Kingdom of Heaven. When you walk with God, you walk in *Light*.

Abraham, Keeper of the Way of the LORD

Before Moses and David, God through a declaration, gave Abraham the grace to walk with Him: "When Abram was ninety-nine years old, the Lord appeared to Abram and said to him, "I am Almighty God; *walk* before Me and be blameless." (Genesis 17:1)

The term *"before me"* is translated from the Hebrew root word *"Paneem"* (פָּנִים), which means *"Faces."* This Hebrew word is also used for the term *"Presence"* of God. So, when it says Adam and Eve hid from the Presence of God (*Genesis 3:8*), it means they hid from the *"faces"* of God! Why faces in plural? Because the word *"Paneem"* can also be translated as *"aspects."*

The Cambridge Dictionary defines *aspects* with the following nouns, *"direction...appearance"* and *"a particular feature or way of thinking...."*

Therefore, when we are asking for his Presence, we are asking for his Faces meaning *His direction (where He is looking), His appearance (facial appearance - Prophetic, Apostolic, etc.), or His way of thinking (His thoughts)* as well. Abraham was given the grace to walk before God's Face(s) or in his Presence. The term *"be blameless"* is translated from the Hebrew word *"Tamim"* (תָּמִים), which also means, *"complete, unblemished or perfect."*

To walk before God's Face means to walk with Him as his Face leads and guides you. God's ways are in his Face i.e., in *His Presence*. As Abraham walked with the Presence of God, the Way (*pathway*) in which he walked was perfect! There is a *Way* in the Presence in which to walk. When Abraham was given this grace to know the *Way* in which he would walk, it was revealed to him to perfectly walk before the Face of God. God's Face has *Light*. That is why we pray, *"…The LORD make His Face shine upon you…."* That means the LORD makes *Light* come off his face towards you. When the *Light of his Face* shines on you, you get favor! "In the light of the king's face is life, And his favor is like a cloud of the latter rain." (Proverbs 16:15)

So, for Abraham to walk before his face meant Abraham walked in the *Light of his Face*. So, Abraham walked and enjoyed God's favor whenever he went. As mentioned above, God must show us his ways and teach us his paths so that we can walk with Him as those are the ways and paths He walks on. Remember, this is God's Wisdom, which He has ordained for believers. It is simple because He is the one teaching us, not a man! As Moses and David both requested that God show them his way(s) and paths, it is evident in *Genesis 18* below that God had shown his way to Abraham. "For I have known him, in order that he may command his children and his household after him, that they keep the way of the LORD, to do righteousness and justice, that the Lord may bring to Abraham what He has spoken to him." (Genesis 18:19)

The grace to walk with God was given to Abraham in *Genesis 17:1*. In Genesis 18, God is speaking well of Abraham that not only is he keeping the *Way of the LORD*, but he commands his children and household to keep it. Abraham had shared this revelation with his children and his household. The Way of the LORD is very significant. First let me explain the term *"Lord"* in the verse above, which is purposefully not translated correctly in English. The term *"LORD"* is used to veil God's Name (יְהוָה). This Name is highly revered in the Hebrew culture due to the following verse: "You shall not take the *name of the Lord* (יְהוָה) your God in vain, for the Lord (יְהוָה) will not hold him guiltless who takes His Name in vain." (Exodus 20:7)

Revealing the Way of the LORD (Derek YHWH)

According to Jewish tradition, this was the name pronounced by the High Priest during the Day of Atonement or *Yom Kippur,* the Holiest Day in the Torah. As such, in order not to take the Name of God in vain because of the above verse, Jewish tradition has veiled the Name of God by substituting it with the terms, *Hashem (The Name)* or the Name *Adonai* while Christians use the term Yahweh, which is close but not accurate either. As Yahweh is familiar to most, we will use it in the proceeding passages. This Name has been veiled in most Bibles by substituting it with the term *"LORD."* This is significant in that Abraham was keeping the *Way of YHWH* (יְהוָה).

Though I have learned through some Biblical scholars I respect, this is not the correct pronunciation of his Name as a good study of the Hebrew Scriptures can reveal this, I will still use the term "YHWH" in reverence for his Name and because it is familiar to most people. In Hebrew, the *Way of the LORD* is the term *"Derek YHWH"* (דֶּרֶךְ יְהוָה). Abraham received a monumental revelation. He was trusted with knowing the way. Abraham walked in the *Way of YHWH.*

Therefore, Abraham was called the *friend of God* as he walked with God. A friend walks with you where you walk! "...Are You not our God, who drove out the inhabitants of this land before Your people Israel, and gave it to the descendants of Abraham Your friend forever?" (2 Chronicles 20:6-8) "And the Scripture was fulfilled which says, "Abraham believed God, and it was accounted to him for righteousness." *And he was called the friend of God."* (James 2:22–24)

God shows his friends what He is doing. "No longer do I call you servants, for *a servant does not know what his master is doing*; but I have called *you friends,* for all things that I heard from My Father *I have made known to you."* (John 15:15) Now you see how the following verse is possible: "And *Enoch walked with God; and he was not, for God took him."* (Genesis 5:24) It is very important to walk with God daily, to know Him, and to know his ways.

Abraham the Guardian and the New Testament Connection

Abraham was such a friend of God that whatever was precious to God, Abraham saw as precious. So, when he was given the revelation of the way of the LORD, he commanded his household to *"keep it."* When you look at both passages below, the English word *"guard"* and *"keep,"* were both translated from the same Hebrew word *"Shamar* (רָמַשׁ)*,"* which means to *"keep, watch, preserve."* "So, He drove out the man; and He placed cherubim at the east of the garden of Eden, and a flaming sword which turned every way, to *guard* (Shamar) *the Way* to the *Tree of Life."* (Genesis 3:24)

"For I have known him, in order that he may command his children and his household after him, that they *keep* (Shamar) *the Way* of the LORD, to do righteousness and justice, that the Lord may bring to Abraham what He has spoken to him." (Genesis 18:19) Abraham commanded his household to *guard* the way of the LORD like the cherubim and the Flaming Sword guarding the *Way to the Tree of Life*. No wonder, later Moses and David were asking God to show them his ways. They wanted to walk with Him like Abraham and Enoch. They wanted to walk the same pathways. The same *"Derek YHWH."* If something is being guarded, you need special knowledge of it and access.

In the New Testament, the way of the LORD, which was previously guarded was finally *revealed*. Two scriptures in two distinct parts of the Bible; one in the book of Genesis and the other, in the New Testament book of Acts reveal an amazing but previously veiled truth. As you can see below, Abraham in the Torah and a man named Apollos in the New Testament had one thing in common; they both knew what the entire Bible refers to as "…*the Way of the Lord*.…"

"Now a certain Jew named Apollos, born at Alexandria, an eloquent man and mighty in the Scriptures, came to Ephesus. This man had been instructed in the way of the Lord; and being fervent in spirit, he spoke and taught accurately the things of the Lord, though he knew only the baptism of John." (Acts 18:24–25)

The *knowledge* of the way of the Lord was not only pleasing to God about Abraham that God would bring to him that which He had spoken, but also gave credence to Apollos' teaching *"…accurately the things of God…"* even though he did not have a full grasp of the New Testament revelation. Apollos had been *"…instructed in the Way of the Lord.…"* In two contrasting Biblical times, one mystery was understood with two separate results:

Abraham who was given the revelation of the way and God was pleased with him because he *commanded* his family *to guard* the way of the Lord and Apollos, a man who was *instructed* in the way of the Lord, which helped him *teach accurately* the things of the Lord. By knowing the way of the Lord, Abraham walked blameless before God. By being instructed in the way of the Lord, Apollos was an *accurate teacher* of the things of God.

The knowledge of the way of the Lord will propel you to walk blameless before God in friendship and if you are instructed in it when you teach, you will teach accurately the things of God!

Jeremiah's Great and Foolish Men

As the Bible teaches us, the nation of Israel was birthed from Jacob, Abraham's grandson, whose Father was Abraham's son, Isaac. Abraham commanded, *"...his children and his household after him, they keep the Way of the Lord...."* As such, the command Abraham gave his children would be passed down from Isaac to Jacob and the twelve tribes of Israel from generation to generation. However, over time, it becomes obvious that the knowledge of the way was lost or forgotten.

By Moses' generation, this knowledge may have been lost in Egypt among Abraham's descendants as Moses, the chosen deliverer of Israel requested God to *show him* his ways. The Bible notes that God did show Moses his ways but to the children of Israel, He showed them his acts. The children of Israel saw the miracles (acts) but did not know God's ways. *"He made known His Ways to Moses, His acts to the children of Israel"* (Psalm 103:7)

As God does not show favorites, I am convinced God showed Moses and the children of Israel, what they desired to see at the time. Moses wanted to know Him while the children of Israel wanted to see his acts like those they saw when they were delivered from bondage in Egypt. They both received what was necessary: Moses, *His Ways* and the children, *His Acts.* However, God was grieved that though they saw his Acts, their hearts strayed as they did not know his ways as he notes below. He wanted them to know both his ways and his acts.

"Do not harden your hearts, as in the rebellion, As in the day of trial in the wilderness, When your fathers tested Me; They tried Me, *though they saw My work.* For forty years I was grieved with that generation, And said, 'It is a people who go astray in their hearts, *And they do not know My ways.'* So, I swore in My wrath, 'They shall not enter My rest.'" (Psalm 95:8–11)

Like Abraham, Moses must have guarded the way of the Lord after it was *revealed* to him. The Prophet Jeremiah gives us a hint of the loss of Abraham's revelation being passed *thoroughly* from generation to generation as he notes that *some* do not know the way of the Lord. "Therefore, I said, "Surely these are poor. They are foolish; For they do not know the way of the Lord, The judgment of their God. I will go to the great men and speak to them, For they have known the way of the Lord, The judgment of their God." But these have altogether broken the yoke And burst the bonds." (Jeremiah 5:4-5)

Jeremiah makes sure to mention that those who *do not* know the way of the Lord are *"...poor. They are foolish..."* and those who have *known* the way of the Lord are *"...great men...."* Jeremiah also gives us a hint of what the way of the Lord could be defined as; it turns out it is also known as *"...the Judgment of their God...."* This will make sense later: it is all good news!

The great men Jeremiah talks about are like King David, who as shown earlier, requested God to show him his ways and it is obvious from some of the Psalms David wrote that God had revealed his ways to Him. In later passages, we will confirm that King David received a full revelation of the way of the Lord.

Making Straight the Way of the LORD

We are also confronted with another reality: the revelation Abraham gave his children was *changed* through the generations. This is evident when the Tanakh indicates that God planned to send a person who would *"prepare"* the way of the Lord by making it, *"straight."* This shows that some who successfully passed Abraham's revelation may have *perverted* it or made it *crooked* over time. "They have corrupted themselves; They are not His children, Because of their blemish: *A perverse and crooked generation.*" (Deuteronomy 32:5)

In the above verse, the word *"perverse"* is translated from the Hebrew word 'iqqesh' (עִקֵּשׁ), which also means *'twisted.'* And the word *"crooked"* is translated from the Hebrew word 'pethaltol' (פְּתַלְתֹּל). This Hebrew word comes from the root word, 'pathal' (פָּתַל), which means *'to twist.'* So, the verse means that generation *corrupted* themselves because of this *'blemish.'* Because their work was *"to twist"* things that were handed to them, they became *"twisted"*. As they were twisted, they twisted the revelation of the way of the Lord, which was passed down from Abraham causing them to forget it. "A voice was heard on the desolate heights, Weeping and supplications of the children of Israel. For *they have perverted their way;* They have forgotten the Lord their God." (Jeremiah 3:21)

The word *"perverted"* above is translated from the Hebrew word, *"Avah"* (עָוָה), which means *"to bend, twist or make crooked."* Bear in mind the word *avah* shares the same root as the word *"Avon"* (עָוֹן), which is translated as *"Iniquity."* So, iniquity comes from *twisting and distorting truths*. When you continually pervert the ways of God, your fruit is iniquity. The consequences of iniquity are separation from God: "But *your iniquities have separated you from God*: And your sins have hidden His face from you," (Isaiah 59:2) They twisted, bent, or made their way crooked. "From those *who leave the path of uprightness* To *Walk in the ways of darkness;* Who rejoice in doing evil, And delight in the perversity of the wicked; Whose *ways are crooked*, and who are *devious in their paths.*" (Proverbs 2:13–15)

The purpose of this twisting is to *'turn aside'* or *'depart'* from the way(s) of the Lord, as it is said above, they are *"…devious in their paths.…"* The word devious is translated from the Hebrew word *'luz'* (לוּז), which means *'to depart.'*

In the New Testament, Paul deals with a person purposely doing this. "Then Saul, who also is called Paul, filled with the Holy Spirit, looked intently at him and said, "O full of all deceit and all fraud, you son of the devil, you enemy of all righteousness, will you not cease *perverting the straight ways of the Lord*?" (Acts 13:9–10)

The word *"perverting"* in the above verse is the Greek word, *"Diastrepho"* (διαστρέφω), which also means to *"distort, twist, oppose or corrupt."* How is this possible? Through untaught and unstable people twisting God's truth or revelation from generation to generation. In the New Testament, the Apostle Peter highlights what was happening with the revelations God had given the Apostle Paul: "and consider that the longsuffering of our Lord is salvation—as also our beloved brother Paul, according to the wisdom given to him, has written to you, as also in all his epistles, speaking in them of these things, in which are some things hard to understand, *which untaught and unstable people twist to their own destruction*, as they do also *the rest of the Scriptures.*" (2 Peter 3:15–16)

There is nothing worse than being on the receiving end of a very important life-changing message that has been altered or twisted from its original content, intent or emptied of its power to change your life. And to add insult to injury, the twisted message is to purposely get you to depart from the Lord. Indeed, in life it is possible in any culture to inherit lies and pass them down through the generations. It is possible to *"inherit lies"* even from the most trusted of *"fathers"* in a nation's history. Jeremiah highlights this very thing that the *Gentiles* (non-Jews) would discover:

"O Lord, my strength and my fortress, My refuge in the day of affliction, The Gentiles shall come to You From the ends of the earth and say, *"Surely our fathers have inherited lies*, Worthlessness and unprofitable things." (Jeremiah 16:19)

The revelation of the way of the Lord had to be passed down in its *original state* as that which Abraham received from God: nothing more, nothing less! The authentic revelation of the way of the Lord had to be passed down through well taught and stable people who considered it as precious as Abraham and *guarded it* against perversion from generation to generation. As we mentioned earlier, Apollos was *"…instructed in the Way of the Lord…."* However, this did not happen over time. As such, out of his great love, God had to send the Prophet Isaiah to prophesy that *'a Voice'* would cry out in the wilderness (*a land of dryness*) of the nation of Israel; he would be a voice sent to *prepare* the way of the Lord. "The voice of one crying in the wilderness: "Prepare the way of the Lord; *Make straight* in the desert A highway for our God." (Isaiah 40:3)

As earlier I had mentioned the *"pathways"* of God, the verse above calls this pathway a *"highway,"* which is significant. God also sent Malachi to confirm Isaiah's announcement about a *"Messenger"* God would send to prepare the way of the Lord. "Behold, I send My messenger, And he will *prepare the Way* before Me. And the Lord, whom you seek, Will suddenly come to His temple, Even the Messenger of the covenant, In whom you delight. Behold, He is coming," Says the Lord of hosts." (Malachi 3:1)

Please note, the Hebrew word translated in the English text as *"Prepare"* in the two passages above is the word *"Panah"* (פָּנָה), which means *"To Turn"* and the Hebrew word translated in the English text as *"Straight"* in Isaiah 40:3 above, is the word, *"Yashar"* (יָשַׁר), which means to *"to be straight, smooth, even, right or make pleasant or prosperous."* As such, God was sending a voice to *"turn"* the way of the Lord back to its original intent, how it is supposed to be *and* to make it smooth, even, straight, pleasant, or prosperous from its present condition of perversion or crookedness.

The Tanakh does not reveal this messenger. However, the New Testament Book of Matthew reveals this *Voice* or *Messenger* of God as none other than John, commonly known as *the Baptist* (or Immerser). "In those days John the Baptist came preaching in the wilderness of Judea, and saying, "Repent, for the kingdom of heaven is at hand!" For this is he who was spoken of by the prophet Isaiah, saying: "The voice of one crying in the wilderness: 'Prepare the way of the Lord; Make His Paths straight.'" (Matthew 3:1–3)

As mentioned earlier, the paths are those that *"branch out of"* the major road or way. As such, John was to prepare (*Panah: "to turn"*) the way of the Lord and to straighten (Yashar: *"make right"*) the paths that *"branch out"* of the way of the Lord! The way had been made crooked and was in a perverted state. John was meant to *turn it* and *straighten it.*

In the New Testament Book of John, John the Immerser confirmed that he was indeed the voice crying out in the wilderness.

"Now *this is the testimony of John,* when the Jews sent priests and Levites from Jerusalem to ask him, "Who are you?" He confessed, and did not deny, but confessed, "I am not the Christ." And they asked him, "What then? Are you Elijah?" He said, "I am not." "Are you the Prophet?" And he answered, "No." Then they said to him, "Who are you, that we may give an answer to those who sent us? What do you say about yourself?" He said: "I am 'The voice of one crying in the wilderness: "Make straight the way of the Lord,"' as the prophet Isaiah said." (John 1:19–23)

John was not only entrusted with guarding the way but now there seemed to be a change. God chose John to be the one *turning people* towards the way of the Lord. He was entrusted withstanding at the gate of the way and heralding people to know that where he was standing was the way. He was the voice heralding the people to the correct gate.

They had been going another way and thought they were on the right path, but their direction was wrong, and their path was crooked. This gate had been guarded since Adam's days and only those who were granted the privilege to walk in his way had seen it. But now a voice sent by God was here to herald the people to come to the correct gate and walk down the straightway that God had ordained for them to walk.

This was so monumental that Yeshua said the following about John: "This is he of whom it is written: 'Behold, *I send My messenger* before Your face, *Who will prepare Your way before You.*' 28 For I say to you, among those born of women *there is not a greater prophet than John the Baptist;* but he who is least in the kingdom of God is greater than he." (Luke 7:27–28)

Why does He say this?

Because John was a demarcation: He was a boundary line! He was a voice that would cause a shift like no other up to that point in human history! As Yeshua says: "For *all the Prophets* and *the law prophesied until John.*

And if you are willing to receive it, *he is Elijah who is to come.*" (Matthew 11:13-14)

Please note that Yeshua did not say the *Prophets* and *the Law* were done away with. He said they *"...prophesied until John...."* Yeshua highlights that if you could receive it, John was coming in the spirit of Elijah, the one to *"turn"* hearts as prophesied by Malachi:

"Behold, I will send you Elijah the prophet Before the coming of the great and dreadful day of the Lord. 6 And *he will turn The hearts* of the fathers to the children, And the hearts of the children to their fathers..." (Malachi 4:5–6)

So, the importance of John cannot be underestimated. He was the voice that began an extraordinary time: *"The law and the Prophets were until John. Since that time, the kingdom of God has been preached, and everyone is pressing into it."* (Luke 16:16)

The law and prophets *prophesied until John*, then since that time, the *Kingdom of God was at hand,* and everyone was *"pressing"* into it. Because John prepared the way of the Lord and made it straight, Yeshua says in *Luke 7:28,* "*...among those born of women there is not a greater prophet than John the Baptist."* Since John *remained* at the gate of the way he had made straight, and everyone was now entering the Kingdom passing him, Yeshua concludes *"...he who is least in the kingdom of God is greater than he."* John's only mission was to prepare the way, not enter it.

"Tevilah Teshuva":
Preparing the Way and Making It Straight

As surely as the prophets, Isaiah and Malachi had prophesied, John began his ministry by *"turning"* the children of Israel as he preached, *"Repent, for the Kingdom of Heaven is at hand..."* according to *Matthew 3:1*. The word noted in English as *"Repent"* is translated from the Greek word, *metanoia;* which means, *"changing the mind"* or *"change in the inner man."* Also, the Hebrew word *"shuv"* (בוש), which is translated as *"Repent"* in English (as *used in Ezekiel 14:6*) means to *"turn back"* or *"return."* John was preaching a message that encouraged the people to *"turn"* their minds and hearts towards the *Kingdom of Heaven* as what they kept through tradition or what had been passed down through the ages was not accurate.

John is also tasked with making the way *"Straight"* as it had been perverted or changed. Remember, Abraham was given the revelation of the way of the Lord about four hundred years before the Torah of Moses was given to the children of Israel on Mount Sinai. As such, John came preaching a revelation that Abraham understood and received before the detailed Law of Moses: "And he went into all the region around the Jordan, preaching a baptism of repentance for the remission of sins" (Luke 3:3).

The Torah mentions in *Exodus 30:17-21*, *Leviticus 8:7* and extensively in *Numbers 19* the process of *"purification"* by *"washing"* with water. The Hebrew word used in most of these passages is the word *"rachatz"* (רחץ), which means to wash. This is different from a *full-body immersion*. However, when Naaman *"dipped"* himself seven times in the Jordan in 2 Kings 5:14, the Hebrew word used for *dipped* is from the root word *"Taval"* (טבל), which means to be fully immersed.

Though not specified in the Torah, full immersion was practiced as it is shown in the following passage: "For the Pharisees and all the Jews do not eat unless they wash their hands in a special way, holding the tradition of the elders. When they come from the marketplace, they do not eat unless *they wash*. And there are many other things which they have received and hold, like the *washing* of cups, pitchers, copper vessels, and couches." (Mark 7:3-4)

The phrase, "...*they wash*..." in verse 4 is translated from the Greek word, *"baptizó"* (βαπτίζω), which means to fully immerse. So, when they came from the marketplace, they did not eat unless they were immersed in water. This is referred to as the *"immersion of purification"* in many Jewish writings. The Hebrew word for this immersion of purification is *"Tevilah"* (טְבִילָה), whose root word is *Taval*. In Jewish teachings, the two words for Baptism (*Tevilah*) and Repentance (*Teshuva*) are normally separated in discussions.

However, there is no mention of a merging of the two words to form the phrase *"Tevilah Teshuva."* The phrase *"Tevilah Teshuva"* (*Baptism of Repentance*) is not a normal topic discussed because it was not mentioned in the Torah. Therefore, it is important to note that John preached a new concept: a *Baptism of Repentance* for the exact purpose of *remitting sins*.

Abram the Hebrew and John the Immerser

As mentioned previously, the Hebrew word for the English word *"Hebrew"* in the above passage is *"Ivri"* (ירבע), which according to the famous Torah commentator, *Rashi (Rabbi Shlomo Yitzchaki)* means "...*the one who came from the other side* (רֵבֵע) *of the river (Euphrates)…*[1] or what I would call "*one from beyond the other side.*" Rashi uses the Hebrew word *"avar"* (רֵבֵע), for *"other side"* which means *"passed,"* as in pass over. As Abram was following God's voice and moved from his homeland towards the land God promised him, his journey involved God guiding him from one side of a river(s) to the other side. The river was a physical boundary but was also a spiritual line of demarcation for God as He notes that if Abraham and his family were on the below *"…other side of the river…"* they *"…served other gods…."*

"And Joshua said to all the people, "Thus says the Lord God of Israel: 'Your fathers, including Terah, the father of Abraham and the father of Nahor, dwelt *on the other side of the River* in old times; and *they served other gods.* Then I took your father Abraham *from the other side of the River,* led him throughout all the land of Canaan, and multiplied his descendants and gave him Isaac." (Joshua 24:2–3)

In the United States of America, there is an idiom used to describe one's social-economic status by mentioning he/she grew up or is from the *"other side of the tracks.."* This is because many towns used to be or are still socially and economically divided along the *railroad tracks* running through them. The railroad tracks were a social-economic boundary within the community for some towns or cities e.g., families in neighborhoods located on the south side of the trains tracks of Town "A" could be struggling financially while families in neighborhoods in the same Town A located on the Northside of the train's tracks could be prospering financially.

As such, in Abraham's case, the rivers not only acted as boundaries between kingdoms or peoples but also determined their *belief systems.* The Jordan river was a spiritual demarcation line. So, God had to move Abraham and the children of Israel to the *"other side"* of the Jordan River so that they could *"turn"* their hearts towards Him by putting away *other gods.* Joshua describes this vividly below:

"Then I brought your fathers out of Egypt, and you came to the sea; and the Egyptians pursued your fathers with chariots and horsemen to the Red Sea. So, they cried out to the Lord; and He put darkness between you and the Egyptians, brought the sea upon them, and covered them. And your eyes saw what I did in Egypt. Then you dwelt in the wilderness a long time. And I brought you into the land of the Amorites, *who dwelt on the other side of the Jordan,* and they fought with you. But I gave them into your hand, that you might possess their land, and I destroyed them from

---

1. Rosenbaum and Silbermann, *Rashi on Genesis 14:13 & 42:8.*

before you. Then Balak the son of Zippor, king of Moab, arose to make war against Israel, and sent and called Balaam the son of Beor to curse you. But I would not listen to Balaam; therefore, he continued to bless you. So, I delivered you out of his hand. *Then you went over the Jordan and came to Jericho.* And the men of Jericho fought against you—also the Amorites, the Perizzites, the Canaanites, the Hittites, the Girgashites, the Hivites, and the Jebusites. But I delivered them into your hand. I sent the hornet before you which drove them out from before you, also the two kings of the Amorites, but not with your sword or with your bow. I have given you a land for which you did not labor, and cities which you did not build, and you dwell in them; you eat of the vineyards and olive groves which you did not plant.' "Now therefore, fear the Lord, serve Him in sincerity and in truth, and *put away the gods which your fathers served on the other side of the River* and in Egypt. *Serve the LORD*! And if it seems evil to you to serve the LORD, choose for yourselves this day whom you will serve, whether the gods which your fathers served *that were on the other side of the River,* or the gods of the Amorites, in whose land you dwell. But as for me and my house, we will serve the LORD." (Joshua 24:6–15)

Joshua concludes by letting them know the purpose of his sermon: "Now therefore," he said, "*put away the foreign gods* which are among you and *incline your heart* to the LORD God of Israel." (Joshua 24:23)

The English word *"incline"* in the above passage is translated from the Hebrew word *"natah"* (נָטָה), which means *"to TURN, incline or bend."* Therefore, a *"Hebrew"* is a person whom God has brought *"...from the other side of the river...,"* who has put away foreign gods and whose heart is *"inclined"* or *"turned"* towards God, to serve Him and obey his voice! That is why Abram was introduced in the Torah as the *first Hebrew*; God took him *from the other side of the river* (Jordan) so that he would put away the foreign gods and *turn his heart* towards Him. Abram was a beginning of a people that God would take from the *other side of the river* so that they could put away the foreign gods and turn their hearts towards Him, obey his voice and to serve Him. When God made Abraham and his descendants cross the rivers, they went through *"River Crossings of Turning"* to become those known as *Hebrews* or *"Irvrim"* (עברים).

As such, God told Moses to introduce Himself in preparation for what He was about to do: "Then they will heed your voice; and you shall come, you and the elders of Israel, to the king of Egypt; and you shall say to him, '*The* LORD *God of the Hebrews* has met with us; and now, please, let us go three days' journey into the wilderness, that we may sacrifice to the Lord our God.'" (Exodus 3:18–19)

Why did God call them Hebrews before Moses' deliverance? As descendants of Abraham, in God's Eyes, they were Hebrews. Through Abraham, God had moved them from the *"other side."* Their Fathers were already Hebrews when they entered Egypt in Joseph's generation and due to many being born and raised in Egypt for over four hundred years, God gave them a national *"baptism"* when they walked through the *Sea of Reeds* (or what is commonly referred to as the *Red Sea*) on their way to Mount Sinai. "Moreover, brethren, I do not want you to be unaware that all our fathers were under the cloud, all passed through the sea, *all were baptized into Moses in the cloud and in the sea*," (1 Corinthians 10:1–2)

As you know, Joshua also led the children of Israel through the river Jordan: "So it was, when the people set out from their camp to cross over the Jordan, with the priests bearing the ark of the covenant before the people, and as those who bore the ark came to the Jordan, and the feet of the priests who bore the ark dipped in the edge of the water (for the Jordan overflows all its banks during the whole time of harvest), that the waters which came down from upstream stood still, and rose in a heap very far away [e]at Adam, the city that is beside Zaretan. So, the waters that went down into the Sea of the Arabah, the Salt Sea, failed, and were cut off; and the people crossed over opposite Jericho. Then the priests who bore the ark of the covenant of the LORD stood firm on dry ground in the midst of the Jordan; and all Israel crossed over on dry ground, until all the people had crossed completely over the Jordan." (Joshua 3:14–17)

This was a *spiritual baptism* for the generation Joshua led, just like Moses led the children of Israel through the Red Sea. By going through, the Jordan river, they were immersed to turn their hearts.

So, the similarity here between Abram the Hebrew and John the Immerser was the *"Turning"* of the heart and mind towards God *by water*. The connection between Abram the Hebrew and John the Immerser was the revelation of *the Way of the Lord*: one was given the revelation and he passed it to his family with the command *to guard* it, but it got lost and perverted through the generations, while the other received the revelation and was entrusted to *correct it* and pass it on again to the children of Israel.

Revealing the Way of the LORD (Derek YHWH)
John's *Tevilah Teshuva* and the Will of God

Let us discuss the phrase *"Baptism of Repentance."* The word translated in English as *"Baptism"* is the Greek word, *"Baptisma"* (βάπτισμα), which means *"submerging"* or *"dipping/immersion."* The word noted in English as *"Repentance"* is translated from the same Greek word for "Repent": *metanoia* (μετανοέω); which means, *"changing the mind"* or *"change in the inner man."*

Recall the Hebrew word for Repent is *"shuv"* (שׁוּב), which means *"to turn back."* This is amazing! John was proclaiming an *"immersion for the changing of the mind or inner man or turning back the heart."* The person would get submerged in water and their mind or inner man would be supernaturally changed towards repentance *"...for the remission of sins..."*! "And he went into all the region around the Jordan, preaching a baptism of repentance for the remission of sins," (Luke 3:3)

The English word *"for"* in the above verse is translated from the Greek word *"eis"* (εἰς), which implies *"to a particular purpose or result"* while the English word *"remission"* is translated from the Greek word *"aphesis"* (ἄφεσις), which means *"dismissal, release, fugitively a pardon or complete forgiveness."* Therefore, the *result* of John's immersion was the dismissal or complete forgiveness of sins! This was the ultimate Breaking News!

Remember in the Torah, confession of sin involved the person making atonement for their sin in the form of a trespass offering: "And it shall be, when he is guilty in any of these matters, that he shall *confess that he has sinned* in that thing; and he shall *bring his trespass offering* to the Lord for his sin which he has committed, a female from the flock, a lamb, or a kid of the goats as a sin offering. So, *the priest shall make atonement for him concerning his sin.*" (Leviticus 5:5–6)

As a result of John's message, two amazing things happened. First, there was an overwhelming response to the message as *all* in the land of Judea and those from Jerusalem went out to him. "John came baptizing in the wilderness and preaching a baptism of repentance for the remission of sins. Then *all the land of Judea, and those from Jerusalem*, went out to him and were *all baptized by him* in the Jordan River, confessing their sins." (Mark 1:4–5)

Please note, again to emphasize: *"...all in the land of Judea..."* and *"...those from Jerusalem..."* went to him and *"...all were baptized by him..."*! Secondly, those who were baptized did something unheard of at the time; they *confessed* their sins without a priest or an offering for atonement.

"Then all the land of Judea, and those from Jerusalem, went out to him and were all baptized by him in the Jordan River, confessing their sins." (Mark 1:5) "Then Jerusalem, all Judea, and all the region around the Jordan went out to him and were baptized by him in the Jordan, confessing their sins." (Matthew 3:5-6)

Here was a revelatory message proclaiming the *remission of sins* through a full water immersion! The result was multitudes confessing their sins and being baptized. Please understand the word *"confessing"* in the above passages is the Greek word *"exomologeó"* (ἐξομολογέω), which, comes from two Greek words, *"ex"* (ἐκ) (from, from out of) and *"homologeó"* (ὁμολογέω) (to speak the same, to agree) which means *"from speaking the same/from agreeing"* as opposed to the usual understanding of confessing as a person detailing all their sins.

They spoke the same thing as what they had been told would be the result of the baptism: the remission of their sins! Can you picture in your mind the news spreading without TV or social media to all in the Judea region and Jerusalem that a man was announcing the remission of sins by water baptism? This caused such an uproar that some from Jerusalem sent *Priests* and *Levites* who went to see John to inquire if he was indeed *"the Prophet"* Moses had mentioned in the Torah (in Deuteronomy 18:15 & 18) who they had been waiting for: "Now this is the testimony of John, when the Jews sent priests and Levites from Jerusalem to ask him, "Who are you?..." ... And they asked him, "What then? Are you Elijah?" He said, "I am not." "Are you the Prophet?" And he answered, "No." ..." (John 1:19-21)

Despite the overwhelming response to John's message by the people in Judea and Jerusalem and visitations from the Priests and Levites coming from Jerusalem, as noted below, the *Pharisees* and *lawyers* (experts in the *Law* of Moses) rejected John's baptism. "But the Pharisees and lawyers *rejected the will of God* for themselves, not having been baptized by him." (Luke 7:30)

Interestingly, the above verse notes that by rejecting John's baptism, they *rejected the Will Of God!* As you may recall, John was preaching a Baptism of Repentance for the remission of sins: that was God's will for all the people. As noted in the New Testament, Yeshua was noted for always seeking God's Will as He stated "I can of Myself do nothing. As I hear, I judge; and My judgment is righteous, because *I do not seek My own will but the will of the Father who sent Me.*" (John 5:30)

As such, if Luke 7:30 mentioned in the previous passage states that the baptism of John was *the Will of God*, it would be expected that Yeshua knowing God's will would show up at John's baptism and be baptized. Please notice that when He did show up, He waited until "...*all the people*..." had been baptized then He came to John to be baptized. "When *all the people* were baptized, it came to pass that *Jesus also was baptized*; and while He prayed, the heaven was opened." (Luke 3:21)

The Immersion of Repentance and the fulfillment of all Righteousness

What is significant about the meeting between John and Yeshua was that John genuinely felt Yeshua was supposed to baptize him. However, Yeshua revealed to John what this was all about. "Then Jesus came from Galilee to John at the Jordan to be baptized by him. And John tried to prevent Him, saying, "I need to be baptized by You, and are You coming to me?" But Jesus answered and said to him, "Permit it to be so now, for thus it is fitting for us to fulfill all righteousness." Then he allowed Him." (Matthew 3:13–15)

Yeshua revealed to John that his baptism of repentance *fulfills all righteousness*! Wow! Watch this carefully! The word *"fulfill"* is translated from the Greek word, *"pleroo"* (πληρόω), which means to *"fulfill, meet or complete."* The function of John's baptism was to begin or prepare the *completion* of all righteousness! Let us recap: Abraham commanded his household to "...*keep the Way of the Lord*...": "For I have known him, in order that he may command his children and his household after him, that they keep the way of the Lord, to do righteousness and justice, that the Lord may bring to Abraham what He has spoken to him." (Genesis 18:19)

Remember, the Prophet Isaiah prophesied about the *"Voice"* who would come to *"prepare the Way of the Lord."* "The voice of one crying in the wilderness: "Prepare the way of the Lord; Make straight in the desert A highway for our God." (Isaiah 40:3)

We verified that John the Baptist was confirmed as the *"Voice"* whom Isaiah and Malachi had prophesied about because he confirmed it himself: "Then they said to him, "Who are you, that we may give an answer to those who sent us? What do you say about yourself?" He said: "I am 'The voice of one crying in the wilderness: "Make straight the way of the Lord,"' as the prophet Isaiah said." (John 1:22–23)

In addition, John's message was specifically about turning the hearts of the people to God and paying attention to the nearness of the Kingdom of Heaven: "In those days John the Baptist came preaching in the wilderness of Judea, and saying, "Repent, for the kingdom of heaven is at hand!" (Matthew 3:1–2)

If John was preparing the way of the Lord, then his baptism was *the* preparation. And now Yeshua just revealed something significant: He states that this baptism or *His* baptism was to *"…fulfill all righteousness…."* So, the preparation of the *fulfillment* of all righteousness was this baptism of repentance for the forgiveness of sins!

John's Immersion and the Kingdom of God

To understand where this is leading, we must look at interesting statements Yeshua made in the following passage to Nicodemus, a Jewish ruler from the Pharisees who came to see Him at night.

"There was a man of the Pharisees named Nicodemus, a ruler of the Jews. This man came to Jesus by night and said to Him, "Rabbi, we know that You are a teacher come from God; for no one can do these signs that You do unless God is with him." Jesus answered and said to him, "Most assuredly, I say to you, *unless one is born again, he cannot see the kingdom of God.*" Nicodemus said to Him, "How can a man be born when he is old? Can he enter a second time into his mother's womb and be born?" Jesus answered, "Most assuredly, I say to you, *unless one is born of water and the Spirit, he cannot enter the kingdom of God*. That which is born of the flesh is flesh, and that which is born of the Spirit is spirit. Do not marvel that I said to you, 'You must be born again.' The wind blows where it wishes, and you hear the sound of it, but cannot tell where it comes from and where it goes. So, is everyone who is born of the Spirit." Nicodemus answered and said to Him, "How can these things be?" Jesus answered and said to him, "Are you the teacher of Israel, and do not know these things?" (John 3:1–6)

The statement I want to highlight is this, *"…unless one is born of Water and the Spirit, he cannot enter the kingdom of God…."* So, to enter the Kingdom of God, you must be *"born"* of Water and the Spirit. The Greek word translated as *"born"* in this verse is *"gennao"* (γεννάω), which means *"begotten"* or *"birthed."* The Greek word translated *as "enter"* is *"eiserchomai"* (εἰσέρχομαι), which is *"enter, go into or come into."* Therefore, John's immersion in water or *"water baptism"* was one of two required steps of being *"birthed"* or being *"begotten"* into the Kingdom of God! The second step of entering the Kingdom of God is being born of the Spirit as noted by the passage below: "When He had been baptized, Jesus came up immediately from the water; and behold, the heavens were opened to Him, and He saw the Spirit of God descending like a dove and alighting upon Him. And suddenly a voice came from heaven, saying, "This is My beloved Son, in whom I am well pleased." (Matthew 3:16–17)

Yeshua had just explained to Nicodemus what He, Himself had experienced. With John's baptism, He demonstrated the *rebirth* in the *immersion of Water* and the Spirit. That is why John preached about the *"Kingdom of Heaven is at hand"* to propel the people to fulfill the first step of being born (rebirthed) to be able to enter the Kingdom of God. There was a *Way* to enter the Kingdom of God, but it had to be done by first *"…fulfilling all righteousness…"* through John's water baptism first! A person must be righteous to enter the Kingdom of God!

Yeshua, The Revealer of the Way of the Lord

As concluded in the previous passages, the way of the Lord had become a sealed-up and guarded mystery over time. God sent John the Baptist to prepare it for its proper revealing and manifestation. After the preparation, Yeshua came to finally reveal the way of the Lord. In His own words: "For John came to you *in the Way of Righteousness*, and you did not believe him; but tax collectors and harlots believed him; and when you saw it, you did not afterward relent and believe him." (Matthew 21:32)

Remember, John was the voice who came to *prepare* and *straighten* the *"Way of the Lord."* In one sentence, Yeshua equates what John was doing to the *Way of Righteousness*! What did John do? He prepared the people by preaching to them to *"…repent for the Kingdom of God is at hand…"* and turning their hearts through the water baptism and remitting their sins. So, the *revelation* of this book is this: *the Way Of the Lord is the Way Of Righteousness*. Through his baptism, he opened the "way of righteousness" pointing toward the *One Who* would bring righteousness to the people through the "Spirit" and "Fire"

"Now as the people were in expectation, and all reasoned in their hearts about John, whether he was the Christ or not, John answered, saying to all, "I indeed baptize you with water; but *One* mightier than I is coming, whose sandal strap I am not worthy to lose. *He will baptize you with the*

Holy Spirit and fire. His winnowing fan is in His hand, and He will thoroughly clean out His threshing floor, and gather the wheat into His barn; but the chaff He will burn with unquenchable fire." (Luke 3:15–17)

Do you see why Abraham guarded this? It was guarded because it had to be *revealed*: "The LORD has made known His Salvation; His Righteousness *He has revealed* in the sight of the nations." (Psalm 98:2)

It says He has "...*made known His Salvation...*" Many Christians know about Salvation. However, righteousness must be *"revealed"* because it is hidden. The word *"revealed"* in the above verse is translated from the Hebrew word, *"galah"* (גָּלָה), which means *"to uncover."* God's righteousness must be *uncovered* by God Himself. Why? Because He veiled it. Unless God reveals his righteousness, we cannot find it. Every culture in the world searches for God's righteousness. Because they have failed on their own to find it, they have produced their own. That explains the *myriads* upon *myriads* of religions and doctrines trying to find *enlightenment*. How do we know He veiled it? Because of the following verse: "So, He drove out the man; and He placed cherubim at the east of the garden of Eden, and a flaming sword which turned every way, to guard *the Way to the Tree of Life*..." (Genesis 3:24)

The cherubim and the flaming sword were guarding *the Way* to the *Tree of Life*. "In the way of righteousness *is life*, And in its pathway, there is no death." (Proverbs 12:28) They were guarding the way of righteousness, where the tree of life can be found! Even if you passed the cherubim, you would encounter a flaming sword. But what is the *function* of the cherubim? The following verses give us a clue: "Make one cherub at one end, and the other cherub at the other end; you shall make the cherubim at the two ends of it of one piece with the mercy seat. And the cherubim shall stretch out their wings above, *covering the mercy seat with their wings*, and they shall face one another; the faces of the cherubim shall be toward the mercy seat." (Exodus 25:19–20)

The cherubim "...*stretch out their wings*...." for this purpose: "...*covering the mercy seat with their wings*...." The word *"covering"* is translated from the Hebrew word, *"sachechim"* (סֹכְכִים), which has the same Hebrew root as the Hebrew word, *"mesakim"* (מָסַכִּים), which means *"screens."* The cherubim's wings would *cover like a screen*! That is why they were part of the designs on the "curtains" and on the *"veil"* as you can see: "Moreover you shall make the tabernacle with ten *curtains* of fine woven linen and blue, purple, and scarlet thread; with artistic *designs of cherubim*, you shall weave them." (Exodus 26:1) "You shall make *a veil* woven of blue, purple, and scarlet thread, and fine woven linen. It shall be woven with an artistic *design of cherubim*." (Exodus 26:31)

The cherubim's wings function as a *screen* or *veil*. To see God Who sits on the Mercy Seat, the Priest had to see behind the veil representing the covering wings of the cherubim. "The cherubim spread out their wings above and covered the mercy seat with their wings. They faced one another; the faces of the cherubim were toward the mercy seat." (Exodus 37:9)

For Ezekiel to be able to see, God positioned Himself "...*above the head of the cherubim...*" (Ezekiel 10:1), otherwise, God was known as "...*the One Who dwells between the cherubim...*" (2 Kings 19:15, Psalm 99:1, etc.). If HE is between the cherubim, you cannot see Him as he is *veiled* by the wings of the cherubim. The wings of the cherubim show that they stand as a *screen* between dimensions. They are guardians of the dimensions of God. If their wings are down, you will see what is usually behind them. If their wings are up, you will not see into the next dimension.

Therefore, when God put cherubim "...*at the east of the garden of Eden...,*" He put them there as a veil to the door of "...*the was....*" The phrase *"East"* in the above verse is translated from the Hebrew word, *"Qedem"* (קֶדֶם), which is not about a compass direction. That Hebrew word is translated as *"aforetime, ancient time, before, be in front"* i.e., in the beginning. In modern Hebrew, it is translated as *"precede."* The cherubim *"veiled"* the Way to the Tree of Life, which preceded "time." It was there at the beginning. Whatever is at the beginning is a foundation or a pattern. The flaming sword kept you physically out if you passed the veil.

This way to the tree of life *exists in the "aforetime"* or in what I call *"...the was..."* as it says, "...*You are righteous, O LORD, The One Who is and Who Was and Who is to be...*" (Revelation 16:5). To explain it in the simplest of terms, God exists in those three (not exclusively) dimensions i.e., *Who Was* (aforetime), *Who Is* (present time) and *Who Is to be* (future). These are dimensions, that all exist simultaneously. The way to the tree of life exists in *"...Who Was...."* The way of the Lord or the way to the tree of life is one of those called *"the ancient paths"* as it exists in *"...the Was..."*:

"...they have caused themselves to stumble in their ways, From *the ancient paths,* To walk in pathways and not on a highway," (Jeremiah 18:15) As this path is veiled by cherubim, God must reveal it! Revelation comes only when God allows the cherubim to lift their wings to release what comes out of God or what He has hidden. "It is the glory of God to conceal a matter, But the glory of Kings to search out a matter." (Proverbs 25:2)

If the way of righteousness is life, which is the same as the way of the lord, it means Abraham was guarding this revelation like the cherubim and the flaming sword. This is what Moses and David wanted to know and find: *The Way*, which was guarded from the beginning! Notice what David says: "*Lead me,* O Lord, in Your righteousness because of my enemies; *Make Your Way straight* before my face." (Psalm 5:8)

David understood God makes your way straight when He *leads* you into his righteousness! From the beginning, God was *leading Abraham into His Righteousness*. Abraham was a man of faith who was gifted righteousness by God, and he became a Righteous man. He was a righteous man because God gifted him righteousness. *This is the Way of the Lord; it is the Way of Righteousness.* This righteousness gifted by God was *revealed* to Abraham. "…the Righteousness of God *is revealed* from faith to faith; as it is written, "The just shall live by faith." (Romans 1:17)

Man cannot by himself become righteous without Divine revelation: it must be revealed. "Where there is *no Revelation*, the people cast off restraint; …" (Proverbs 29:18) Without revelation from God, the people have cast off restraint with *methods* of becoming righteous. Ask anyone what they must do to become righteous, and you will get a million ways, methods, steps, and principles, including anything from smoking cannabis, meditations, positive thinking, floggings, pilgrimages, refusing modernity, denying foods, to some crucifying themselves. The manufactured lists can be exhausting.

Man cannot by himself become righteous without instruction from God: "A man who *wanders from the way of understanding* will rest in the assembly of the dead." (Proverbs 21:16) The word *"understanding"* in the above verse is translated from the Hebrew word, *"haskel"* (הַשְׂכֵּל), which means *"to study, to learn."* This comes from the Hebrew root word, *"sakal"* (שָׂכַל), meaning *"intelligence."* So, the *"way of understanding"* means the way to become intelligent through study or learning.

So, a man who wanders from the *way of study* or learning will rest in the assembly of the dead! Why study? "O LORD, I know *the way of man* is not in himself; *it is not in man who walks to direct his own steps.*" (Jeremiah 10:23) Wow! Jeremiah says it is *"…not in man…to direct his own steps…."* We do not have it in ourselves to be righteous on our own. We need instruction; we need to learn! We need revelation. But from whom does man learn? From God: "A man's steps are of the LORD; How can a man understand *his own way?*" (Proverbs 20:24)

We do not have it in us to understand (learn) our way. Over the generations, we think somehow, we have figured it out without God. We hunger and thirst for a righteousness that excludes God. We do this by ascribing to ourselves righteousness that comes from *what we do.*

For example, we may feel we are good in our eyes because we are responsible citizens who may have never committed a crime, have a great career, are very highly educated, volunteer for all good causes, have no debt, have good credit, we have invested well, we pay all their bills on time, we pay our taxes, we faithfully vote, we take care of our families, we love in a nice neighborhood, etc. All of these could qualify for the phrase, "…*he/she was a good man/woman because he/she did all these things*…." There is nothing wrong with doing good things and having great achievements.

All these things seem right to us, but they do not *qualify* us for righteousness. Whatever things one may *"do"* to feel *"right,"* still lead to the grave. "There is a way that seems right to a man, but its end is the *way of death."* (Proverbs 16:25) Only God can lead you to righteousness and his way of righteousness leads to life: a life where there is no death. It is Him Who leads you into the way and once you have found it by his leading, He gifts it to you, and you become what you naturally hunger for: "Blessed are those who hunger and thirst for righteousness, For they shall be filled." (Matthew 5:6)

If you hunger and thirst for true righteousness, you will be filled. How do you get filled? Exactly like how Abraham was filled: "And he believed in the LORD, and He accounted it to him for Righteousness." (Genesis 15:6) God filled Abraham with righteousness and Abraham became a righteous man. "For the LORD is Righteous, He love righteousness" (Psalm 11:7) God is the *Righteous One* Who gives righteousness to us: that is the way of the Lord. If God loves righteousness and He gives you righteousness, how can't He love you?

Chapter 3

The Blessing for All the Families on the Earth

The Convergence of the Gospel

"The light of the eyes rejoices the heart, And a good report makes the bones healthy" (Proverbs 15:30). The phrase *"...makes the bones healthy..."* is translated from the Hebrew word *"dashen"* (דָּשֵׁן), which means to *"...grow fat...."* This Hebrew word is the same word from which the phrase *"...will be made rich..."* in the following verse: "The generous soul *will be made rich*, And he who waters will also be watered himself." (Proverbs 11:25) The good news is delightful for humanity.

"How beautiful upon the mountains Are the feet of him who brings *good news*, Who proclaims peace, Who brings glad tidings of good things, *Who proclaims salvation*, Who says to Zion, "Your God reigns!" (Isaiah 52:7)

The phrase *'good news'* is translated from the Hebrew word *"mebaser"* (מְבַשֵּׂר), which comes from the root word, *"baser"* (בָּשַׂר) meaning *"herald"* i.e., a messenger or forerunner who comes with an enthusiastically good announcement of an event about to come. That is why the messenger's feet are *beautiful* because wherever he goes, he brings good news. As noted by the Prophet Isaiah, this messenger brings *"...glad tidings of good things, who proclaims salvation...."*

In the preaching of the *"Gospel"* (good news), the message of *"Salvation"* is always the main and at most times the only theme emphasized in church. But that is only half of the message as there is another crucial ingredient missing! When preaching the Gospel, we preach that Yeshua came to bring us Salvation; to save us from our sins as we are told, *"...and you shall call His name JESUS, for He will save His people from their sins."* (Matthew 1:21).

The name Yeshua is the English translation of the Greek Name *"Iésous"* ('Ιησοῦς). This Greek Name *"Iésous"* is a transliteration of the Hebrew name *"Yeshua"* (ישוע), which means *"Salvation."* It is fitting therefore to note that the angel said, *"...and you shall call His name Jesus, for He will save His people from their sins...."* As his Name shows, Yeshua came to bring us salvation from our sins. He has made known his salvation, but He also came to *unveil* the way of the Lord. He came to *"reveal"* the way of the Lord.

To be precise, He also came to *reveal the Way of Righteousness*. "Oh, sing to the LORD a new song! For He has done marvelous things, his right hand and his holy arm have gained Him the victory. *The* LORD *has made known His salvation; His righteousness He has revealed* in the sight of the nations." (Psalm 98:1–3) The LORD has made known his Yeshua (Salvation). But also, He has *revealed* his righteousness in the *"...sight of the nations...."* This is on full display for the entire world to see. This is available to all nations. Therefore, to herald the *"...marvelous things..."* God has done, we must share the *fullness* of the Gospel; we must announce that *His Salvation is now known (in Yeshua) and the Righteousness of God has now been revealed (by Yeshua).*

Yeshua revealed that the way of the Lord is indeed the way of righteousness. *In Yeshua, Salvation has been manifested and in Him the Way of Righteousness been revealed: This is the Gospel!* "For I am not ashamed of the gospel for *it is the power of God to salvation* for everyone who believes, for the Jew first and also for the Greek. *For in it the righteousness of God is revealed* from faith to faith; as it is written, "The just shall live by faith." (Romans 1:16–17)

Paul says above, the Gospel *"...is the power of God to Salvation..."* i.e., the power of God *to Yeshua* for every believing Jews and Greek (nations). For this message to get to its *"full power,"* it must be preached with two ingredients: that *Yeshua came to bring us Salvation from our sins* but also *to reveal* the *Righteousness of God* in us! As it says, *"For in it..."* that is, *inside* of this powerful Divine message, *"...the righteousness of God is revealed...."*

God had already planned to know we could not be righteous on our own and we were incapable of saving ourselves: "Listen to Me, you stubborn-hearted, who are far from righteousness; I bring My Righteousness near, it shall not be far off; My Salvation shall not delay..." (Isaiah 46:12–13)

The discerning ones caught a glimpse of this good news. The Psalmists were already heralding it: "My mouth shall tell of *Your Righteousness and Your Salvation* all day For I do not know their limits." (Psalms 71:15) "I have proclaimed the *Good News of Righteousness* in the great assembly; indeed, I do not restrain my lips, O LORD, You Yourself know." (Psalms 40:9) His righteousness is no longer far; it is here! His salvation has already arrived!

Why is this crucial to include the revelation of his righteousness in this Gospel? Because of this: "to demonstrate at the present time His righteousness, that *He might be just* and the *justifier of the one who has faith in Jesus.*" (Romans 3:26)

In the above verse, the word "Just" is used in the place of the word righteous. But both words are used interchangeably because righteousness and justice are intertwined. "*Righteousness* and *Justice* are the foundation of Your throne; Mercy and truth go before Your face." (Psalm 89:14)

The two words have to do with part of the operation of the Kingdom of God. God is a king and a judge, who is righteous and just. Because he is righteous and just, He as the king and judge can use the laws of his kingdom to declare you righteous. Which laws? *The law of Faith and the law of Righteousness.*

The Law of Faith and the Law of Righteousness

The law of faith nullifies all boasting based on what we do to become righteous. This is a spiritual law set in the Kingdom of God.

"Where is boasting then? It is excluded. By what law? Of works? No, but *by the law of faith*. Therefore, we conclude that a man is justified *(declared Righteous) by faith* apart from the deeds of the law." (Romans 3:27–28) The law is this: "*...a man is declared righteous by faith....*" Therefore, if anyone were to go into God's courtroom before the *"Judgement Seat"* to justify themselves or declare themselves righteous because of the things they have done, the books will be opened, and the law of faith will judge them. What does this mean? If the person's righteousness was not attained by Faith through God or if their righteousness was not received from God as a *gift*, the law of Faith will nullify their claims. I can imagine the summary sounding something like, *"...This court hereby declares that you are not righteous according to the Laws of the Kingdom of God..."*

The Torah and prophets talked about this form of righteousness. Abraham received righteousness apart from his deeds. "For the promise that he would be the heir of the world was not to Abraham or to his seed through the law, but through the righteousness of faith." (Romans 4:13) Abraham is the father of our belief in God. So, we are to imitate him in this and as *One Who* through faith inherited the promises of God. "...but imitate those who through faith and patience inherit the promises. For when God made a promise to Abraham because He could swear by no one greater, He swore by Himself, saying, "Surely blessing I will bless you, and multiplying I will multiply you. "And so, after he had patiently endured, he obtained the promise." (Hebrews 6:12–15)

By us reading and learning about Abraham, the Torah presents righteousness that comes from God, which is apart from our deeds and works. "But now the righteousness of God apart from the law is revealed, being witnessed by the Law and the Prophets" (Romans 3:21) But even after the Law and the Prophets, it is clear there is a righteousness of God through faith in Jesus Christ: "even the righteousness of God, through faith in Jesus Christ, to all and on all who believe. For there is no difference..." (Romans 3:22)

Interestingly, the writer says, *"...there is no difference...."* No difference in what? There is no difference between the *righteousness of God apart from the law*, which Abraham obtained through faith, and the *Righteousness of God through faith in Jesus Christ,* which we have attained. It is the same righteousness! The same righteousness was given two ways: *"by faith"* and *"through faith."* "Since there is one God who will justify the circumcised *by faith* and the uncircumcised *through faith*." (Romans 3:30)

So, there is no difference between the two methods because it is a *GIFT* given freely through God's grace and received with the *gift of faith*! As it goes on to say: "...for all have sinned and fall short of the glory of God, being justified freely by His grace through the redemption that is in Christ Jesus, whom God set forth as a propitiation by His blood, through faith, to demonstrate His righteousness, because in His forbearance God had passed over the sins that were previously committed, to demonstrate at the present time His righteousness, that He might be just and the justifier of the one who has faith in Jesus." (Romans 3:23–26)

As we are no longer in the early days of Abraham, God had to *"...demonstrate His righteousness..."* to us all. For Abraham had divine revelation on diverse aspects, which he passed down to his children and we still study them to this day. But to us, how were we to know this righteousness unless it was revealed to us through *demonstration* by God?

This does not even do it justice but imagine being guilty of a very serious crime, the Jury has found you guilty of all charges and the Judge has sentenced you to death. You could *appeal* the judgment to *justify yourself*. You appeal by providing more information about *your deeds* to prove you are innocent. However, the Judge reminds you of a law that states *One innocent man, freely and willingly presented himself to the Court to take your place and any other that is ever guilty.* Because He shed his blood on your behalf, you can be exonerated of all charges as though you never committed them.

Your guilty record in the Court would be exchanged with an innocent man's record and you could leave the courtroom with that man's innocence on record. You have a choice: serve your sentence or accept this "grace" for your redemption. If you believed in the law, you would be set free. The Court is in the *Kingdom of Heaven*, The Judge *is God*, the *One* innocent Man *is Yeshua*, and the Law the Judge references is called *the Law of Faith*.

The *law of Faith* was already present in the Kingdom of Heaven from the beginning. *Righteousness by faith* was already available from the beginning as even *Abel* was considered righteous. "By faith Abel offered to God a more excellent sacrifice than Cain, through which he obtained witness that he was righteous." (Hebrews 11:4)

Yeshua was there before the foundation of the world. Therefore, when Adam fell, God had to *demonstrate* his righteousness to us since Adam had picked up *his own righteousness* from the tree. It should be that because you are righteous, you do good deeds! However, that tree reversed this and caused us to think that it is through our deeds that we become us righteous. So, because of Adam's doing: "There is none righteous, no, not one." (Romans 3:10)

There was none! Even Abraham had his righteousness given to him by God! For those who trust that their deeds would make them righteous, here is a truth: "Now we know that whatever the law says, it says to those who are under the law, that every mouth may be stopped, and *all the world* may become guilty before God." (Romans 3:19) All deeds done to make us righteous make us guilty. That is, the *entire world* in that courtroom would be guilty! Why? "Therefore, by the deeds of the law *no flesh will be justified in His sight,* for by the law is the knowledge of sin." (Romans 3:20)

So, imagine your appeal and you are listing all the *honorable deeds* you did to prove your innocence. There will still be a prosecutor who will list his/her *"...knowledge of sin..."* that you committed and is on record. In his wisdom and his Grace, God set forth Messiah Yeshua as a *"mercy seat"* by whose blood (instead of that of animals) we would receive redemption. Yeshua's sacrifice was set forth by God to *"...to demonstrate at the present time His Righteousness...."* God was demonstrating a righteousness that only comes from Him, not from us and our deeds. "...that He might be just and the justifier of the one who has faith in Jesus." (Romans 3:26)

God, He is the *Righteous One*: "In His days Judah will be saved, And Israel will dwell safely; Now this is His name by which He will be called: *The Lord our Righteousness.*" (Jeremiah 23:6) HE is also the *One Who* makes you Righteous: "Or is He the God of the Jews only? Is He not also the God of the Gentiles? Yes, of the Gentiles also, since *there is One God* who will *justify the circumcised by faith* and *the uncircumcised through faith*." So, our conclusion must be the same as Paul's conclusion: "Therefore we conclude that a man is justified by faith apart from the deeds of the law." (Romans 3:28)

The revelation of God's righteousness then grows *"...from faith to faith...."*

God's Will: *His Way of Righteousness*

The will of God was for all people to walk in the way of the Lord so that they could enter the Kingdom of God. Again, you cannot enter the Kingdom of God without being baptized in water. So, John's baptism was the first step onto the *Way of Righteousness:* this was the will of God. As such, those who rejected the message and refused to be baptized by John were out of the will of God! As noted previously, this was the fate of the Pharisees and lawyers: "But the Pharisees and lawyers rejected the will of God for themselves, not having been baptized by him." (Luke 7:30)

If the Will of God was for all to be baptized as a step to enter the Kingdom of God, Yeshua admonishes us with the following: "Not everyone who says to Me, 'Lord, Lord,' shall *enter the kingdom of heaven,* but he who *does the will* of My Father in heaven." (Matthew 7:21)

As noted above, entering the Kingdom of Heaven must be done according to God's *"Will."* Most will choose *'another'* way, but their way or path of righteousness will not be sufficient because they will not have a righteousness, which is according to God's *'Way of Righteousness.'* That is why Yeshua says this about those who rejected John's baptism: "For I say to you, that *unless your righteousness exceeds the righteousness* of the scribes and Pharisees, you will by no means *enter* the kingdom of heaven." (Matthew 5:20)

The Scribes and Pharisees rejected John's message and baptism because they already had their own righteousness! The English word *"exceeds"* above was translated from the Greek word *"pleión"* (πλείων), which means, *"more excellent"* or *"very great."* Therefore, Yeshua was stating that unless your righteousness was *more excellent* or much greater than the righteousness of the Scribes and Pharisees, you were in trouble. How could your righteousness be more excellent than theirs? First, you must know Yeshua indicates there were two types of righteousness: one the Scribes and Pharisees had and another which exceeds the former. Here is the key: the Scribes and Pharisees were walking in *their own righteousness*!

Let me explain. Recall, that God had already sent John to prepare the way and make it straight! The children of Israel were not walking in the way of righteousness that leads to Life. Instead, they were walking in their *"own"* righteousness, so that is why John was sent! John baptized all in Judea, recall Yeshua said it was for the fulfillment of *"all"* righteousness. So, when the Scribes and Pharisees rejected John's baptism; they rejected the way of righteousness from God and refused to *"turn"* from their own crooked way! That is why Yeshua was saying unless the righteousness you have is more excellent than the righteousness the Scribes and Pharisees were walking in, you could not enter the Kingdom of Heaven. You cannot *"enter"* the Kingdom of Heaven with your own righteousness because it will *always be insufficient* as it is not according to God's Will. Therefore: "But we are all like an unclean thing, And *all our righteousness's are like filthy rags;*" (Isaiah 64:6)

All righteousness that comes from man in any form is like *filthy rags. Our Righteousness must come from God alone.* So, Yeshua was letting us know that our righteousness must be more excellent than the righteousness of the Scribes and Pharisees because theirs was like filthy rags, not being from God. So, what is the more excellent righteousness? Paul explains perfectly what Yeshua was saying:

The Blessing for All the Families on the Earth

"Brethren, my heart's desire, and prayer to God for Israel is that they may be saved. For I bear them witness that they have a zeal for God, but not according to knowledge. For they *being ignorant of God's righteousness*, and *seeking to establish their own righteousness, have not submitted to the righteousness of God*." (Romans 10:1–3)

Because they were ignorant of God's righteousness, they established *their own righteousness*! The word *"established"* in the above verse is translated from the Greek word *"histémi"* (ἵστημι), which means *"cause to stand, hold up."* They have stood in their own righteousness. How can they be ignorant of God's righteousness? They have *"...zeal for God...."* Aren't they the most *zealous* scholars and teachers of the Torah? Paul does not doubt that they were zealous for God, for indeed he says they are zealous *"...but not according to knowledge...."* Where did their knowledge fail?

In this: "Every word of God is pure; He is a shield to those who put their faith in Him. *Do not add to His words*, Lest He rebuke you, and you be found a liar." (Proverbs 30:5–6) They were ignorant of God's righteousness because it was guarded. This was not automatically *revealed* because they had to have a desire to seek it from God instead of devising their own system. This happened by violating the above command, *"...Do not add to His words...."* By adding to God's words, they formed *traditions*, which were handed down from generation to generation that were not from God. Therefore, they exchanged *the knowledge of God* for the *traditions of men*. They passed down the *commandments of men* rather than the commandments of God. "Therefore, the Lord said: "Inasmuch as these people draw near with their mouths And honor Me with their lips, But have removed their hearts far from Me, And their fear toward Me is *taught by the commandment of men*." (Isaiah 29:13)

We see this manifestation with an encounter with Yeshua: "Then the scribes and Pharisees who were from Jerusalem came to Jesus, saying, "Why do Your disciples *transgress the tradition of the elders?* For they do not wash their hands when they eat bread." He answered and said to them, "Why do you also transgress the commandment of God because of your tradition? For God commanded, saying, 'Honor your father and your mother;' and 'He who curses father or mother, let him be put to death.' But you say, 'Whoever says to his father or mother, "Whatever profit you might have received from me is a gift to God"— then he need not honor his father or mother.' *Thus, you have made the commandment of God of no effect by your tradition*. Hypocrites! Well did Isaiah prophesy about you, saying: 'These people draw near to Me with their mouth, And honor Me with their lips, But their heart is far from Me. And in vain they worship Me, *teaching as doctrines the commandments of men.*'" (Matthew 15:1–9)

When they were confronting Yeshua, they were very clear about one thing, *"…Why do Your disciples transgress the tradition of the elders?."* I would have expected them to be more concerned about his disciples *transgressing God's commands.* "For laying aside the commandment of God, you hold the tradition of men—the washing of pitchers and cups, and many other such things you do." He said to them, "All too well *you reject the commandment of God, that you may keep your tradition."* (Mark 7:8–9)

But they saw the traditions of the elders as ways to righteousness! These traditions were *added* to God's Words. Traditions may seem good but if they are added to God's Words and taught as though they come from God, they have the opposite effect. Yeshua says it plainly, *"…Thus you have made the commandment of God of no effect by your tradition….."* Traditions of men taught as though they come from God *nullify God's Word!* A righteousness that comes from the *"…fear…taught by the commandments of men…"* is not a righteousness that comes from God.

When men do this, they have set up their own righteousness, which instead of being light, is *"…filthy rags…."* This is by no means a critique of the children of Israel only as the gentiles (nations) were not any better. Israel had been taught the Torah, but they added to it. The gentiles had absolutely no idea of where to begin. This is symptomatic of human existence: the multitude of so-called paths of righteousness have been devised by man without seeking God.

Paul who said, *"…my heart's desire and prayer to God for Israel is that they may be saved. For I bear them witness that they have a zeal for God, but not according to knowledge…."* (Romans 10:1–2) was speaking from experience: "And I advanced in Judaism beyond many of my contemporaries in my own nation, *being more exceedingly zealous for the traditions of my fathers."* (Galatians 1:14)

Paul had been more zealous for the *"…traditions of my fathers…"* The same Paul also warned about the type of righteousness the gentiles normally seek, which is rooted in the *"basic principles of the world."* These basic principles of the world are *"…the commandments and doctrines of men…":* "Therefore, if you died with Christ *from the basic principles of the world,* why, as though living in the world, do you subject yourselves to regulations "Do not touch, do not taste, do not handle," which all concern things which perish with the using—according to *the commandments and doctrines of men*? These things indeed have an appearance of wisdom in *self-imposed religion,* false humility, and neglect of the body, but are of no value against the indulgence of the flesh." (Colossians 2:20–23)

This is still prevalent today with various *'gurus'* teaching myriads of ways to become righteousness. Most rely on keeping *"traditions of men"* to appear righteous. "Beware lest anyone cheat you through philosophy and empty deceit, *according to the tradition of men*, according to the basic principles of the world, and not according to Christ." (Colossians 2:8)

There is a misconception where people are tempted to think what Paul was saying only applied to Jewish people or those *'under the law'* but for them, since there is *'Grace,'* these scriptures do not apply to them. But God warned the Jewish people long before Paul. "Hear the word which the Lord speaks to you, O house of Israel. Thus says the Lord:

> "Do not learn the way of the Gentiles; Do not be dismayed at the signs of heaven, For the Gentiles are dismayed at them. *For the customs of the peoples are futile.*" (Jeremiah 10:2–3)

God told the Jewish people not to learn *"...the way of the gentiles...."* And He specifically added that *"...the customs of the peoples are futile...."* Why? There are no *'gentile'* customs on the planet that produce righteousness-none! If Yeshua Himself was dealing with Jewish self-righteousness when asking for righteousness exceeding that of the Pharisees, where would He begin with gentiles? God describes our customs as futile!

If you look, the themes for self-righteousness from the verses above are similar:

- *"...taught by the commandment of men..."*
- *"...teaching as doctrines the commandments of men..."*
- *"...you reject the commandment of God, that you may keep your tradition..."*
- *"...exceedingly zealous for the traditions of my fathers..."*
- *"...according to the commandments and doctrines of men..."*
- *"...according to the tradition of men..."*
- *"...according to the basic principles of the world, and not according to Christ...."*
- *"...the customs of the peoples..."*

Everything above has its origin *from men*, not from God! Paul calls these the *"basic principles of the world."* These are things in which people boast, that he summarized as the *"flesh"*:

"For we are the circumcision, who worship God in the Spirit, rejoice in Christ Jesus, and have *no confidence in the flesh*, though I also might have confidence in the flesh. If anyone else thinks he may have confidence in the flesh, I more so: circumcised the eighth day of the stock of Israel, of the tribe of Benjamin, a Hebrew of the Hebrews; concerning the law, a Pharisee; concerning zeal, persecuting the church; concerning the righteousness which is in the law, blameless. But what things were gain to me, *these I have counted loss for Christ*. Yet indeed I also count all things loss for the excellence of the knowledge of Christ Jesus my Lord, for whom I have suffered the loss of all things, and *count them as rubbish*, that I may gain Christ and be found in Him, *not having my own righteousness, which is from the law, but that which is through faith in Christ, the righteousness which is from God by faith;*" (Philippians 3:3–9)

Just like Paul, I can boast in my pedigree, my *tribe* or for this century, 'my race.' Like Paul, I can boast about super-patriotism, my higher education, and my persecution of non-believers who I feel are evil. I can boast of my social media popularity and be influential within my local community. I could boast, but it would be boasting about my *"…confidence in the flesh …."* It is all unclean. Paul counts all of them *"…as rubbish…."* Through centuries of deception and cheating, we have been taught that these things of the flesh are what make you a *good* person.

"Beware lest anyone cheat you through philosophy and empty deceit, according to the tradition of men, according to the basic principles of the world, and *not according to Christ*." (Colossians 2:8) Interestingly, the word, *"principles"* in the above verse is translated from the Greek word *"stoicheion"* (στοιχεῖον), which means *"elements of knowledge."* However, Strong's under 4747 states, *"The RSV however renders stoixeia as "elemental spirits," i.e., spiritual powers or "cosmic spirits" (DNTT, 2, 828). These views 4747 /stoixeíon ("elements") as ancient astral beings associated with the very beginning (make-up) of the earth…"* Therefore, we can say these *"traditions of men"* are according to (or come from) the *"cosmic spirits"* of the world. Imagine that!

So, like Paul, I am willing to suffer *"…the loss of all things…"* and to *"…count them as rubbish…"* that I may *"…gain Christ and be found in Him, not having my own righteousness, which is from the law, but that which is through faith in Christ, the righteousness which is from God by faith…"*? That is a question you should ask yourself. The brightness of God's righteousness in one's life shines according to the level at which he/she has suffered a loss of all things of the flesh to gain Christ and is detangled from the things taught by the *elemental spirits* of the world. That is how you walk blameless.

If you look at Abraham, he walked this way. He left all his philosophies, customs, and traditions of men at the command of God, gave up his family name, prestige, or anything he could *"boast in"* and became fully free to receive and carry the full weight of the righteousness that comes from God. To regard the teachings of cosmic spirits more than the teachings of God, makes us unclean and unrighteous (self-righteous). "But we are all like an unclean thing," (Isaiah 64:6)

More excellent righteousness must come from somewhere other than man himself! It must be a *'Divine Righteousness'* with a Divine origin. It must be a righteousness that God Himself can agree that it is 100 percent genuine because it comes from Him. So, where else can you get this more excellent righteousness than from God Himself? Can anyone's own way of righteousness exceed God's way of righteousness? That is not possible! *"'Can a mortal be more righteous than God? Can a man be more pure than his Maker?"* (Job 4:17)

It would be foolish to answer the above questions with anything other than a No! "Who can bring a clean thing out of an unclean? *No one!* (Job 14:4) There is nothing on, above, and below the earth that any man can do that can exceed God's righteousness. "The heavens declare His righteousness, And all the peoples see His glory." (Psalm 97:6)

The question is do the heavens declare *your* righteousness or God's righteousness? Do they declare the things you boast in? Maybe in one's own eyes, he or she may *feel* righteous through their fleshly efforts but to enter God's Kingdom, a person must pick God's *Way of Righteousness* to enter. Why? God is a king; He is the righteous and just ruler over *His Own Kingdom*.

In a kingdom, you serve a king according to his desire, not by popular vote as in a democracy. The king's opinion is the one that counts. A king does have Counselors to consult but the decision is his alone. Therefore, to enter the kingdom that *belongs* to God, we must follow his criteria for entering, not our own. If John's water baptism were God, the King's will for his people, who would dare rebelliously reject it and suppose they would enter his Kingdom by their own methods?

John's mission was complete; fulfilling what Malachi had stated previously: "Behold, I send My messenger, And he will prepare the way before Me." (Malachi 3:1) He baptized all from Judea and those from Jerusalem and when he was done, he baptized Yeshua in the same manner.

God's Way of Righteousness Is the Judgement of God

If you recall, Jeremiah called the way of the Lord, *the Judgement of the Lord*. "Therefore, I said, "Surely these are poor. They are foolish; For they do not know the way of the Lord, The judgment of their God. I will go to the great men and speak to them, For they have known the way of the Lord, The judgment of their God." But these have altogether broken the yoke And burst the bonds." (Jeremiah 5:4–5)

John came to *"turn"* the nation of Israel to *the Way* God was *going to make them Righteous* as ultimately, that is *His desired Judgment* so that they could *"enter"* the Kingdom of God. Now you understand why Abraham, 430 years before the Law of Moses was given to the children of Israel, was commanding his household to keep the way of the Lord. He understood one thing: God's way of making one righteous was the *only* way to become righteous.

This revelation came to Abraham after God said the following: "And he believed in the LORD, and He accounted it to him for righteousness." (Genesis 15:6) When reading this verse, it should be noted that Abraham did not make himself righteous; God made him righteous! It says, *"…and HE (God) accounted it to him (Abraham)…."*

The word *"accounted"* in the above verse is translated from the Hebrew word *"chashav"* (חָשַׁב). This word seems a bit vague to me considering such an important topic as righteousness. To go deeper, Strong's notes the root of this word means to *"plait or interpenetrate"* or to literally *"weave"* or generally *"fabricate."* That is amazing!

According to The American Heritage Dictionary, here are the definitions of the above words:

- Plait – "to braid"
- Interpenetrate – "to become mixed or united by penetration…to penetrate thoroughly; permeate or pervade…"
- Weave – "to construct by interlacing or interweaving strips or strands of material…"

The Blessing for All the Families on the Earth

- Fabricate – "to make; create"

So please picture this in your imagination: Abraham *believed* in the LORD and God caused *righteousness* to *penetrate him thoroughly, permeating his being, braiding itself through him like interweaving strands to make him Righteous!*

So, imagine righteousness entering the very DNA strands of Abraham! Here is an even greater picture: "Then those who feared the Lord spoke to one another, And the Lord listened and heard them; So, a book of remembrance was written before Him. For those who fear the Lord And who *meditate* on His name." (Malachi 3:16)

The word *"meditate"* from the above verse is translated from the same Hebrew root word *"chashav,"* which was briefly discussed above and previously translated as *accounted*. So, in the above verse, it was translated as *meditate* because the Hebrew root of this word also forms the word translated as *"thought"* (chashav). So, not only did God *account* righteousness to Abraham but HE *thought* Abraham was righteous. Abraham lived from faith to faith *meditating* on his gifted righteousness.

The Hebrew root of *chashav* is also where you get the word *"chashev"* (חָשֵׁב), which means to *"calculate."* So not only did God account righteousness to Abraham, and think Abraham as righteous, He *calculated* Abraham to be righteous. In Math, it is known that Pi (π) is a constant 3.14. Things in the Spiritual realm can be limitless but are *measurable*. So, if righteousness has a constant number, God calculated and made certain that Abraham received the full measure of that constant state of righteousness. Abraham was righteous!

This is God's work! God is the One Who makes you righteous and we must declare this to the world: "The LORD has revealed our righteousness. Come and *let us declare* in Zion *the Work of the LORD our God."* (Jeremiah 5:10) That is why God lets him know the following:

> "....*in you* and *in your seed all* the families of the earth shall be blessed." (Genesis 28:14)

What Abraham received would also be transmitted in his *"seed"* and all the families of the earth shall be blessed. We will go into details later with this; however, the word righteousness needs to be defined to realize the impact of what God did to Abraham.

The Fairness of the Way of the Lord in question

When people are working for something and someone else gets it for free, there will always be resentment and a perception that the system in place is unfair. The Bible even shows God was talking to Ezekiel about the house of Israel's complaint; they found the way of the Lord to be unfair! "Yet you say, 'The way of the Lord is not fair.' Hear now, O house of Israel, is it not My way which is fair, and your ways which are not fair?" (Ezekiel 18:25)

"Yet you say, 'The way of the Lord is not fair.' O house of Israel, I will judge every one of you according to his own ways." (Ezekiel 33:20) The way of the Lord seems unfair only to those that have their own *ways of righteousness* because they have worked very hard building up towers towards Heaven with *'steps'* on how to become righteous. For God asks, *"… is it not My way which is fair, and your ways which are not fair?"* Man's ways are never fair. Imagine if it was given to man to hand out righteousness to their fellow men. Entire populations would be doomed.

In certain places you would only be given righteousness if you were from a certain tribe, race, a specific geographical area, a certain upbringing, a certain social class, weight, height, athleticism, abilities, a certain level of education, among others. We could go on and on with the *"man-made requirements."* But the way of the Lord is fair because the righteousness of God is free! You only must believe it and it is yours!

Unveiling the Word Righteousness

I was taught that a righteous person was in *"right standing with God."* But this phrase was always a snare for me because my next question was always something like, *"So what do I need to "do" to be in right standing with God?."* In my quest to be in right standing, I would then look for materials that would provide me with lists of the things I needed to do to be in right standing with God. As you will discover, this is the very reason God sent the voice in the wilderness crying out to prepare the way of the Lord for the children of Israel.

God's Righteousness

The Hebrew word for righteous is *"Tsedeq"* (צֶדֶק), which is translated as *"rightness"* or *"a perfect and a just weight."* This is the root word for two of

The Blessing for All the Families on the Earth

the following the Hebrew words: *"Tsaddiq"* (צַדִּיק), which is translated as a *"just, righteous person"* and *"Tsedaqah"* (הְקָדָצ), which is translated in English as *"Righteousness."* To understand the word righteousness, we must further search the Greek as the New Testament was also written in Greek. The Greek word for righteous is *"Dikaios"* (δίκαιος) (pronounced-*dik'-ah-yos*) derived from the word *"Dike"* (δίκη), which means *"equitable (in character or act);"* by implication: *innocent, holy (absolutely or relatively).*

The Greek word for righteousness is *"Dikaiosune"* (δικαιοσύνη) (*dik-ah-yos-oo'-nay*), which would be defined as *"God's judicial approval"* or *"divine approval."* But this word *"Dikaiosune"* is also derived from the word *"Dike"*: so, from understanding the two words (*Dikaios* and *Dikaiosune*) and where they are both derived (from *Dike*), I can say God's *"divine approval" comes from a person's "innocence."* However, this innocence must have a measurement, which must be approved by God. Here it is remembered from above, the Hebrew word *"Tsedeq"* means a *"perfect and just weight."*

And we know Who is perfect: *"Therefore you shall be perfect, just as your Father in heaven is perfect."* (Matthew 5:48)

If God is perfect, then He is the *"perfect and just weight"* to measure everything. Meaning we are to *measure our Righteousness according to His Righteousness*, not our own! Therefore, a person's innocence is measured according to *God's innocence* as it is already weighed as *"perfect"* because God is perfect. Therefore, to be righteous or by implication *"innocent,"* the person must have the same *weight of innocence* as God's innocence! I will explain the implications of this statement later.

However, for now, I would like to suggest that the word righteousness (for your imagination) is the *substance of the "innocence of God" i.e., Righteousness is the innocence of God*. Why define it as the innocence of God? Because the Greek word *'Dike,'* which implies *innocence* is the foundation of the word *'Dikaiosune'* (righteousness). It is the simplest definition I could find, which would help me understand the meaning without removing the obvious: righteousness is something I cannot cause, become, have, or try to achieve without God.

Let me explain why this definition makes sense to me as you can see from the following verses righteousness *has a substance*: "Commit your way to the Lord, Trust also in Him, And He shall bring it to pass. *He shall bring forth your righteousness as the light,* And your justice as the noonday." (Psalm 37:5–6) See this in your imagination; righteousness coming forth as a light ray or light beam. *The substance of Righteousness is Light*. Malachi confirmed further in the following verse:

"But to you who fear My name *The Sun of Righteousness* shall arise With healing in His wings; And you shall go out And grow fat like stall-fed calves." (Malachi 4:2) The word *"Sun"* in the above verse in Malachi is the Hebrew word, *"Shemesh,"* which according to Strong's is *"from an unused root meaning to be brilliant; the sun rising; by implication, the east; figuratively, a ray, i.e. (arch.)."* The passage is implying light like the rising Sun: The *Brilliance of Righteousness* or the *Ray of Righteousness*. Therefore, the substance of righteousness is noted to be as or like light.

A person's *"brilliance of righteousness"* is measured according to the brilliance of righteousness within God. So here is the amazing thing: as God is light, He measures and approves the light in you according to his *Light*. Therefore, God and the entire host of heaven know those who are righteous because there is a measurement to go by: your righteousness is measured according to his righteousness. Please understand, that God is *Light*. He is not just light; He is *Pure Light* as the Bible makes it very clear that in Him, there is no darkness or shadow of turning. "…God is light and in Him is no darkness at all." (1 John 1:5)

"…the Father of lights, with whom there is no variation or shadow of turning." (James 1:17) God is the *purest of Light* as there is no iota of darkness in Him! Therefore, as He is untainted, unpolluted, or unblemished, He is *'one hundred percent Pure Light or one hundred percent Righteous (innocent) Light*! So, to be called righteous, a person must be reflecting the same brilliance of pure or innocent Light that is in God. To emphasize the connection between light and innocence, it is interesting the Bible says the following about the *breastplate* worn by the High Priest:

"So, Aaron shall bear the names of the sons of Israel on the breastplate of judgment over his heart, when he goes into the holy place, as a memorial before the LORD continually. And you shall put in the breastplate of judgment the *Urim* and *the Thummim*, and they shall be over Aaron's heart when he goes in before the LORD." (Exodus 28:29–30) In the above passage, the Hebrew word *"Urim"* (אוּרִים) means *"Lights"* and *"Thummim"* (תֻּמִּים) means *"Perfections."* Both words above are in the plural form. The singular word for Urim is *"Ur,"* which means *"Light"* (אוּר) and the singular form of Thummim is *"Tom"* (תֹּם), which means *"Innocence."*

"So, the *Breastplate of Judgement* had two stones, whose spiritual essence was *"Light and Innocence"*: *The Light of Innocence*! This shows righteous judgement. "And do you think this, O man, you who judge those practicing such things, and doing the same, that you will escape the judgment of God? Or do you despise the riches of His goodness, forbearance, and longsuffering, not knowing that the goodness of God leads you to repentance? But in accordance with your hardness and your impenitent heart you are treasuring up for yourself wrath in the day of wrath and revelation of the *righteous judgment of God*, who "will render to each one according to his deeds" (Romans 2:3–6)

"Stand therefore, having girded your waist with truth, having put on the *breastplate of righteousness*, and having shod your feet with the preparation of the gospel of peace." (Ephesians 6:14–15)

So, what happened to Abraham was not just a concept without substance. Picture this in your mind: *God thoroughly penetrated Abraham with the brilliance of the Light of His Righteousness, braided it into his being, weaved it into his DNA so that Abraham was filled fully with the light of the Righteousness of God.* Therefore, being filled with the light of God's righteousness, Abraham became a righteous man.

Now God is the one who *"accounted"* Abraham with righteousness, here is something I want you to fully understand: this was a permanent work. "I know that whatever God does, It shall be forever. Nothing can be added to it, And nothing taken from it. God does it, that men should fear before Him." (Ecclesiastes 3:14)

In addition, the Bible tells us that righteousness is also a *"Robe."* "...He has covered me with the robe of righteousness..." (Isaiah 61:10) This light of righteousness can clothe you. "I put on righteousness, and it clothed me; ..." (Job 29:14) So not only is it *"within"* but also covers you on the outside. It can function as a *Light of Protection*, as *armor* or a *breastplate*: "...by the armor of righteousness on the right hand and on the left" (2 Corinthians 6:7) "Stand therefore, having girded your waist with truth, having put on the breastplate of righteousness" (Ephesians 6:14) Righteousness is the Armor of Light: "...Therefore, let us cast off the works of darkness, and let us put on *the armor of light*." (Romans 13:12)

The Circles of Righteousness

"He restores my soul; He leads me in the paths of righteousness For His name's sake." (Psalm 23:3)

The English word *"paths"* is translated from the Hebrew word, *"Bemagele"* (בְּמַעְגְּלֵי־), which means *"Circles"* as the root of *"bemagele"* is the last three Hebrew letters in the word (...גַל). These three letters form the Hebrew word *"Agol"* (עָגֹל), which means *"round."* So, what David was saying was that the Lord leads him in *"Circles of Righteousness."*

This is interesting considering God as requiring the Prophet to *"make the paths straight."* How do you make a circle *straight*? Well, this is how the Holy Spirit explained it to me. If you get a round rubber band and twist it, you will get a twisted straight rubber band. But to go further, cut the rubber band in one place, then fold the two ends to meet, then twist it entirely. It would look like a Twizzlers Candy!

So, the condition of the way of the Lord looked like a rubber band with two cut ends and twisted instead of a smooth complete circle! So just like a twisted rubber band, when untwisted returns to a straight rubber band with two cut ends, the Lord sent his messenger to make the paths straight by removing the twists. The Lord had chosen Water *Baptism* as the way to remove the twists.

By baptizing people in the Jordan, John was removing the "twists" or perversions. By Baptizing *"...Jerusalem, all Judea, and all the region around the Jordan..."* (Matthew 3:5), the messenger's job was complete. He had removed the twists and made it straight! So, now it was straight like a rod with two ends. However, since it had two cut ends, there was only one way those ends could be mended together to form the full circle again. Remember, it is a *Circle of Righteousness*. So, consider one end is called the *"beginning"* and the other called the *"end"* i.e., the *Aleph* (א) and the *Tav* (ת) or the *Alpha* (ἄλφα) and *Omega* (Ὠ) in Greek, as popularly known. John knew how to remove the twists, i.e., through Baptism, but did not know how to put the ends together to make a circle. There had to be a way to connect *the beginning* and *the end* to create a complete Circle. Since the straightening was done in baptism, also, the completion into a circle had to be in baptism. The Hebrew word used for *baptism pool* is *"Mikveh"* (מִקְוֶה). This Hebrew word comes from the same three-letter root word for the Hebrew word *"tikvah"* (תִּקְוָה), which means *"hope"* and the Hebrew word *"qavah"* (קָוָה), which means *"bind together by twisting."* So, you could say, baptism *is an immersion of water in the hope of binding together the circle of God's righteousness.* So there had to be one more thing that John had to do to bring the two ends together; to baptize Yeshua as He is the One called as follows:

"I am the Alpha and the Omega, the Beginning and the End the First and the Last." (Revelation 22:13)

Only the One Who had *the beginning,* and *the end* could complete the binding of the circle of righteousness: "looking unto Jesus, the author and finisher of our faith" (Hebrews 12:2) When all had been baptized by John, Yeshua came to be baptized. "Then Jesus came from Galilee to John at the Jordan to be baptized by him. And John tried to prevent Him, saying, "I need to be baptized by You, and are You coming to me?" (Matthew 3:13–14)

Yeshua came to bring the ends together to *complete* the Circle of righteousness, therefore fulfilling all righteousness: "Then Jesus came from Galilee to John at the Jordan to be baptized by him. And John tried to prevent Him, saying, "I need to be baptized by You, and are You coming to me?" But Jesus answered and said to him, "Permit it to be so now, for thus it is fitting for us to *fulfill all righteousness*." Then he allowed Him." (Matthew 3:13–15)

As noted earlier, the word *"fulfill"* is translated from the Greek word, *"pleroo,"* which means to *"fulfill, meet or complete."* Yeshua came to be that One to put the two ends together to complete the circle. By being baptized, Yeshua completed the circle of righteousness. "When He had been baptized, Jesus came up immediately from the water; and behold, the heavens were opened to Him, and He saw the Spirit of God descending like a dove and alighting upon Him. And suddenly a voice came from heaven, saying, "This is My beloved Son, in whom I am well pleased." (Matthew 3:16–17)

God was pleased that the path was made straight, and Yeshua completed *the Circle*. As the one Who completed it, He became the fullness of the righteousness of God. This pleased the father. "For Christ is *the end* of the law *for righteousness* to everyone who believes." (Romans 10:4)

As they are *"Circles of Righteousness,"* not one Circle, when we baptize, we are reminded to baptize as follows: "Go therefore and make disciples of all the nations, baptizing them in the name of the Father and of the Son and of the Holy Spirit," (Matthew 28:19) There are three circles of righteousness, one of the Father, of the Son and of the Holy Spirit. With these three, the three-fold cord is complete. "Though one may be overpowered by another, two can withstand him. And *a threefold cord is not quickly broken.*" (Ecclesiastes 4:12)

So, recall David says, *"…He leads me in the paths (circles) of righteousness For His name's sake…"* This was a great revelation as you know David was a prophet (Acts 2:29–30). We can conclude, the baptism of the church *is an immersion of water in the hope of binding you together with the circles of God's righteousness which was completed by Yeshua.*

So how do we know our righteousness from God is fulfilled? Well, there is a response! "The LORD is *well pleased for His righteousness' sake*; He will exalt the law and make it honorable." (Isaiah 42:21) The English phrase *'well pleased'* in the above verse is translated from the Hebrew word *"Chafetz"* (חָפֵץ), whose root is *"desire."* Therefore, God's desire is fulfilled with his righteousness in us. In Hebrew, the above verse says close to this: *"The LORD is well pleased because of His Righteousness...."* So, Yeshua fulfilled all righteousness by receiving God's righteousness when the following happened:

"When He had been baptized, Jesus came up immediately from the water; and behold, the heavens were opened to Him, and He saw *the Spirit of God descending like a dove and alighting upon Him.* And suddenly a voice came from heaven, saying, *"This is My beloved Son, in whom I am well pleased."* (Matthew 3:16–17)

The Spirit of God descending on Yeshua and *'alighting upon Him'* was the evidence of the fulfillment of all righteousness and the response was immediate by God announcing the Sonship of Yeshua and noting, *"...in whom I Am well pleased...."* Why? *"The LORD is well pleased because of His Righteousness...."*

The baptism was the vehicle for preparing the way of righteousness. Yeshua being baptized was the fulfillment of all righteousness, therefore God was pleased with Him because his Spirit was upon Him. The Spirit of God alighting upon Him was the evidence of the righteousness of God in Him because the Spirit of God rests on righteous people. The Spirit of God comes with three realities, which include: "for the kingdom of God is not eating and drinking, but Righteousness and peace and joy *in* the Holy Spirit." (Romans 14:17)

Enoch did not just walk with God only but received the righteousness of God, which pleased God enough to let him go to heaven without dying. "By faith Enoch was taken away so that he did not see death, "and was not found, because God had taken him;" for *before* he was taken *he had this testimony, that he pleased God."* (Hebrews 11:5)

Now I understand this passage above is from the *'faith'* chapter, but I would like to suggest that it was not only because Enoch had faith. Enoch's faith and the *"result of his faith"* are what pleased God. The result of faith is the *Gift of Righteousness*! It says *"...Abraham believed..."* (faith) and the result was *"…it was accounted to him as righteousness…."* The result of completed faith is righteousness! From the same chapter of faith, it says the following:

> *"By faith* Noah, being divinely warned of things not yet seen, moved with godly fear, prepared an ark for the saving of his household, by which he condemned the world and *became heir* of *the righteousness* which is *according to faith."* (Hebrews 11:7)

Your righteousness begins with receiving Salvation and the gift of righteousness from Jesus, who is the *Righteousness of God.*

> "I will greatly rejoice in the LORD, My soul shall be joyful in my God; For He has clothed me with the garments of Salvation, He has covered me with the robe of righteousness…" (Isaiah 61:10)

This righteousness is fulfilled when you are baptized both in water and in the Holy Spirit.

The Predicament of Right Standing with God

To recap, for one to be righteous, that person must be as *Righteous as God* i.e., have the same *untainted brilliance of His innocence.* In other words, to be declared as *"innocent as God,"* one must be as *'innocent as He is,'* at hundred percent! We cannot contest this as one's righteousness ever exceeds God's righteousness. "'Can a mortal be more righteous than God? Can a man be more pure than his Maker?" (Job 4:17) "Moreover, Elihu answered and said: "Do you think this is right? *Do you say, 'My righteousness is more than God's'?"* (Job 35:1–2)

This is where the good news begins. From the very beginning, Adam was created to bear God's image and likeness, which includes his righteousness. "Then God said, "Let Us make man in *Our image,* according to *Our likeness."* The English word *"image"* in the above verse is from the Hebrew word *"tselem"* (צֶלֶם), which means, *"something cut out."* What is interesting is this Hebrew word shares the same root as the Hebrew word *"tzilum"* (צִלּוּם), used in modern Hebrew to describe a *"photograph."* To go even deeper, *tselem* shares the two-letter root word *"tzel"* (צֵל), which means *"shadow."* Therefore, we are supposed to be the living *"photograph"* or *"shadow"* of God. This explains why it says the following:

"He who dwells in the secret place of the Most High shall abide under the shadow of the Almighty (Shaddai)." (Psalm 91:1)

When we see the word *shadow*, we assume there must be something underneath, yet in Hebrew, the word *"under"* is not included in the above verse. Therefore, this verse goes much deeper. This means the one who dwells in the secret place of God will abide *'as'* his photograph, i.e., that person will live as *an image* of Shaddai. According to the Bible, the above psalm is *"...A Prayer of Moses the man of God..."* (Psalm 91).

We all know that Moses spent days on *the mountain of God* and the Torah says in *Exodus 34:29 "...when he came down from the mountain, that Moses did not know that the skin of his face shone..."* The Hebrew says his skin *"...sent out rays..."*! Why? Because the English word *"shone"* was translated from the Hebrew word *"qaran"* (קָרַן), which means *"to send out rays."* So, if spending time on the mountain of God makes Moses come out with rays of Light coming off his skin, then it shows at that moment, he came down walking in the *image* of God or as the verse says, in *"...the shadow of Shaddai."* The only other time this happens is the Bible is during the following: "Now after six days Jesus took Peter, James, and John his brother, led them up a high mountain by themselves: and He transfigured before them. His face shone like the sun and His clothes became as white as the light." (Matthew 17:1-2)

The secret place of God *is in the Mountain of God*. If you dwell there like Moses or Yeshua, your face will shine as you will be walking in the *shadow* or *image* of God! The Hebrew word for *"likeness"* is from the Hebrew word *"Demuth,"* (דְּמוּת), which means *"like resemblance."* So, if we were made in his image and His likeness, our righteousness must be *"something cut out of Him"* and be of *"like resemblance to His."*

This is the *catch-22*: if we stick to the definition of righteousness as the *"...right standing with God...,"* what then do we do to be in right standing? What do we do to have the pure light of righteousness constantly in my being? Considering we know ourselves personally and intimately, there are no lists in this world or on earth that we could complete, achieve or *"do"* to become as *'innocent as God*. Even if you try by doing all the commandments of Moses: "Therefore, by the deeds of the law *no flesh will be justified in His sight*, for by the law is the knowledge of sin."

It takes humility to recognize how difficult it would be to *try* to be as innocent as God by *your own* goodness or acts of whatever you deem is necessary to become his image or his likeness. To save you from all the to-do lists that you would have to accomplish to become righteous, I have good news for you. But first, I must give you a clue about where to find this good news. There is a pattern in Creation according to the Tanakh, which is noted below: "Then God said, "*Let Us make man* in Our image, according to Our likeness;" (Genesis 1:26)

The Creation pattern is this: God is *the One Who Makes* Us in *His* image and likeness! If a man tries to make himself into God's image or likeness, he has a task that will take him through eternity, if that is possible, and even then, he would still be working on it and never succeed. The Creation pattern is clear: *God is the One Who makes you be like Him!* We go according to his way, not our way. "Who shall bring a charge against God's elect? It is God Who Justifies." (Romans 8:33)

We do not justify ourselves. It is God Who justifies! Therefore, the solution to the awkward phrase "right standing with God" is to acknowledge that righteousness can be defined as "*God's justification for believing in Him.*" "But to him *who does not work* but believes on *Him Who justifies* the ungodly, *his faith* is accounted for righteousness." (Romans 4:5) It says, "…*but to him who does not work….*" There is *no work* for God's righteousness. God entirely does it *when you believe.*

"For *with the heart one believes unto righteousness*, and with the mouth confession is made unto salvation." (Romans 10:10) Does that mean since He has made you righteous, you can freely sin? No! Because God has made you righteous, you do not sin. Awake to the reality that you are righteous! Righteous people are full of the light of God's innocence, why pollute it? "*Awake to righteousness, and do not sin;* for some do not have the knowledge of God. I speak this to your shame." (1 Corinthians 15:34)

Unveiling the Blessing of Abraham

"I will bless those who bless you, And I will curse him who curses you; And in you all the families of the earth shall be blessed." (Genesis 12:3) The phrase, "…*shall be blessed*…" is translated from the Hebrew word '*venivreku*' (וְנִבְרְכוּ). The Torah commentary, *Daat Zekenim* (*Opinion of the Elders*) translated by *Eliyah Munk* on Genesis 12:3, states, "…*The root of the word* ונברכו (venivreku) *is the same as that of* מבריך, *to graft….*"[2]

In the Book, *The Way of God*, Rabbi Moshe Chaim Luzzatto, states,

> "…*God's great love and goodness decreed that the branches of other nations still be given a chance. If they so desired, they still had*

---

2. Tosafot, *Daat Zekenim* 12:3.

> *the free choice to tear themselves loose from their own roots, and through their own actions include themselves among the branches of Avraham's family. This is what God meant when He told Avraham (Bereshis 12:3), "All the families of the earth will be blessed through you."*[3]

All three of the above commentaries and others not mentioned, conclude that the blessing of all the families of the earth in Abraham has to do with being *'grafted'* into the branches of Abraham. Interestingly, Paul's writings confirm this understanding, which further explains how God was to bless the families of the earth.

"For if the first fruit is holy, the lump is also holy; and if the root is holy, so are the branches. And if some of the branches were broken off, and you, being a wild olive tree, were grafted in among them, and with them became a partaker of the root and fatness of the olive tree, do not boast against the branches. But if you do boast, remember that you do not support the root, but the root supports you. You will say then, "Branches were broken off that I might be grafted in." Well said. Because of unbelief they were broken off, and you stand by faith. Do not be haughty, but fear. For if God did not spare the natural branches, He may not spare you either. Therefore, consider the goodness and severity of God: on those who fell, severity; but toward you, goodness, if you continue in His goodness. Otherwise, you also will be cut off. And they also if they do not continue in unbelief, will be grafted in, for God is able to graft them in again. For if you were cut out of the olive tree which is wild by nature, and were grafted contrary to nature into a cultivated olive tree, how much more will these, who are natural branches, be grafted into their own olive tree?" (Romans 11:16–24)

As spiritual matters can be complex to understand, God will use things he created to explain reality in the Spirit. In Paul's passage above, the Holy Spirit inspired Paul like other men of God to write the Scriptures, to use the Olive Tree as an illustration of a spiritual reality. Like a family tree that is connected by ancestry and DNA, God started a family of righteous and holy people after Adam's fall. God picked Abram, who He had 'exalted' as a father as that was the meaning of his name. As we have read before: "And he believed in the LORD, and He accounted it to him for righteousness." (Genesis 15:6)

Abram was now righteous, which meant that God had to make a covenant with Abram to make him a *father of many nations.* "As for Me,

---

3. Luzzatto, *The Way of God*, 139.

behold, My covenant is with you, and you shall be a father of many nations. No longer shall your name be called Abram, but your name shall be Abraham; for I have made you a father of many nations. I will make you exceedingly fruitful; and I will make nations of you, and kings shall come from you." (Genesis 17:4-6)

As a *"Father of many nations,"* Abraham was going to be the *"Root"* of this Tree that God was planting on the earth. "...to those who are of the faith of Abraham, who is *the father of us all."* (Romans 4:16) Though Abraham is the Father, God was the Author of his Faith: "...looking unto Jesus, the author and finisher of our faith," (Hebrews 12:2) God mapped out the Tree first, picked Abraham as the Father of it, and gave him the seed. The Father of a family tree must produce the seed from within himself and from that seed come the Roots. "...for in Isaac, your seed shall be called...." (Genesis 15:6) Out of Isaac came Jacob. Out of Jacob came the twelve main branches of this Olive tree, the twelve tribes of Israel.

So, Abraham, Isaac, and Jacob are three roots from whom the twelve branches of this tree came out. As Abraham became righteous through faith, we too have become righteous through faith. By this, God grafted us into the Tree of Abraham among Abraham's branches (the nation of Israel). That is why it says, *"...in you..."* meaning in Abraham or in Abraham's tree, which came from his seed.

"You are sons of the prophets, and of the covenant which God made with our fathers, saying to Abraham, 'And *in your seed* all the families of the earth shall be blessed.'" (Acts 3:25) Isaac is the seed! If you know your family tree does not have *'Isaac son of Abraham,'* your only option is to be *grafted* into this tree because God planted this tree Himself. "The LORD called your name, green olive tree, lovely and of good fruit... "For the Lord of hosts, who planted you...." (Jeremiah 11:16-17)

God is the One who called them a *"...Green Olive Tree..."* and planted the tree. If you had Isaac, son of Abraham in your natural family tree, make sure your branch is still part of the tree because according to Paul, some branches, *"...Because of unbelief they were broken off...."* "The Lord called your name, green olive tree, lovely and of good fruit. With the noise of a great tumult, He has kindled fire on it, *And its branches are broken."* (Jeremiah 11:16)

For those who were not *'natural branches'* but are now grafted in, Paul warns, *"...do not boast against the branches...Do not be haughty, but fear. For if God did not spare the natural branches, He may not spare you either...."*

Meaning God is the one who does the grafting and *pruning*. It is by faith that you stand as a branch in this Tree. Therefore, if the natural branches *"... do not continue in unbelief, will be grafted in, for God is able to graft them in again.* And if we are grafted in *among these branches*, we have become *"...a partaker of the root and fatness of the olive tree ...."*

The Blessing is being *grafted in* and *being a partaker of the root* and fatness of this Olive tree. That is the blessing available to all families on the earth! That is the blessing of Abraham! I know this is completely different from what you have heard on the blessing of Abraham, and you will ask why being grafted into this Tree is special? Because the roots of this tree are not from the ground standing up. They are from Heaven and the Tree is facing down! This tree is planted by the waters in Heaven. As Isaac gave a clue in the *"Blessing"* he gave Jacob:

"Therefore, may God give you Of the dew of heaven, Of the fatness of the earth, And plenty of grain and wine." (Genesis 27:28) The blessing of Abraham comes to you from Heaven. The roots are based in the Heavens. They start from God coming down on earth! The blessing comes from above as, *"...of the dew of heaven...,"* which then translates to, *"...of the fatness of the earth...."* Compare this blessing to the one Isaac gave to Esau, which was in reverse: "Behold, your dwelling shall be of the fatness of the earth, And of the dew of heaven from above." (Genesis 27:39)

God wanted all the families of the earth to be connected to Heaven first, for his will can come down on earth in their lives as it is in Heaven. Therefore, a Heavenly Priest blessed Abraham: Melchizedek (Genesis 14:18 and Hebrews 7), not an earthly one. One person in the Bible who is shown to have been blessed by Abraham's blessing was *Ruth the Moabitess,* who was a gentile by birth. She grafted herself into the Olive tree when she confessed the following: "...For wherever you go, I will go; And wherever you lodge, I will lodge; Your people shall be my people, And your God, my God." (Ruth 1:16) Because of this confession, Ruth was *grafted* into Israel and the result was that she was included in King David's lineage, which was the lineage of the Messiah.

"...Ram begot Amminadab, Amminadab begot Nahshon, and Nahshon begot Salmon. Salmon begot Boaz by Rahab, Boaz begot Obed by *Ruth*, Obed begot Jesse, and Jesse begot David the king. David the king begot Solomon by her who had been the wife of Uriah." (Matthew 1:4–6) What a blessing to be grafted into this Tree and be counted as King David's great grandmother!

The Spirit was meant to be only for those who were promised, i.e., those grafted into the Tree. The Messiah's work was to graft you into this Tree so you can receive the promise of the Spirit through faith: "Christ has redeemed us from the curse of the law, having become a curse for us (for it is written, "Cursed is everyone who hangs on a tree"), that the blessing of Abraham might come upon the Gentiles in Christ Jesus, that we might receive the promise of the Spirit through faith." (Galatians 3:13–14)

Like Ruth, graft yourself in so that you can receive the full measure of the blessing of Abraham.

Chapter 4

The Adam Principle

Adam, The Two voices and the Two Trees

Before going on to fully explain the significance of why Abraham commanded his house to keep the way of the Lord, which we now know is also the way of righteousness, we must understand the impact of eating from the tree of the knowledge of good and evil. Our dilemma all began with Adam choosing *"his way,"* which seemed right to him when he ate from the *Tree of the Knowledge of Good and Evil*. To give you a picture of what happened, I want to remove the thought that there were only two trees to eat from in the garden. I want to make it simply clear that God graciously put Adam in a fully rich and vibrant garden with *"every tree"* that was pleasant to the eyes and good for food.

"The Lord God planted a garden eastward in Eden, and there He put the man whom He had formed. And out of the ground the Lord God *made every tree grow that is pleasant to the sight and good for food."* (Genesis 2:8–9) God then graciously placed the *Tree of Life* right amid the garden: "…The tree of life was also *in the midst of the garden*, and the tree of the knowledge of good and evil." (Genesis 2:9)

The word, *"midst"* in the above verse is from the Hebrew word *"tavek"* (תָּוֶךְ), which means *"center."* So, God put the tree of life right in the center of the garden for them to fully access it from *all* directions and to eat from it freely. But also notice, the tree of the knowledge of good and evil was also placed amid the garden.

God was very specific when He commanded Adam and Eve:

"And the Lord God *commanded* the man, saying, "Of *every tree of the garden you may freely eat; but* of the *tree of the knowledge of good and evil you shall not eat*, for in the day that you eat of it you shall *surely die*." (Genesis 2:16–17) As noted above, God generously gave Adam and Eve several options to choose from with the words "...*every tree of the garden...,*" which included the tree of life amid the garden. Only *One* tree was forbidden.

Adam was given the ability to choose as one made in the image and likeness of God. *But choice is influenced by the voice you are obeying!* As it is noted in the following verse, God brought the creatures to Adam to see what he would call them. Adam had a choice. As you can see, he chose to name every beast of the field and every bird of the air that God put in front of him: "Out of the ground the Lord God formed every beast of the field and every bird of the air and brought them *to Adam to see what he would call them. And whatever Adam called each living creature, that was its name.* So, Adam gave names to all cattle, to the birds of the air, and to every beast of the field. But for Adam there was not found a helper comparable to him." (Genesis 2:19–20)

The beasts of the field and the birds of the air were not named yet until Adam named them. This decision to name the creatures was not arbitrary. Adam named the creatures after God brought them to him. At that moment, he chose to obey and name them all. He could have chosen not to name the animals. He chose the names himself and God accepted the names Adam came up with. Just as God had put the beasts of the field and the birds of the air before Adam, He had to present the two trees. Why? There were two *"voices"* on the earth at the time. God's voice and a serpent. Why was the serpent there? God had put him there as the following verse notes: "*You were in Eden, the garden of God.*" (Ezekiel 28:13)

However, if your read Ezekiel 28:11–19, you will find out how he fell. Why present the two trees amid the garden? Because the two trees represented two forms of righteousness. The tree of life represented the *"Righteousness from God"* and the tree of the knowledge of good and evil represented *"Self-Righteousness."* They were put amid the garden in the East of Eden. "The Lord God planted a garden *eastward in Eden,* and there He put the man whom He had formed." (Genesis 2:8)

Why the East of Eden? As you recall, the phrase *"Eastward"* in the above verse is translated from the Hebrew word, *"Qedem"* (קֶדֶם), which is more than just a direction. It is also translated as *"aforetime, ancient time, before, be in front"* i.e., in the beginning. In Hebrew, this is connected to time, as well as the rising of the Sun: "On the east side, toward the rising of the sun…" (Numbers 2:3)

Why the Sun? It is symbolic of how the Light of God emergences from the East. The Light of God would come from the East; from the *"ancient time"* into Garden, then to the rest of Eden and then the Earth, *"…like a bridegroom coming out of his chamber…"*: "…In them He has set a tabernacle for *the sun, Which is like a bridegroom coming out of his chamber And rejoices like a strong man to run its race. Its rising is from one end of heaven, And its circuit to the other end; And there is nothing hidden from its heat."* (Psalm 19:4–6)

This pattern is shown in Ezekiel's vision. "Afterward he brought me to the gate, the gate that faces toward the east. And behold, the *glory of the God of Israel came from the way of the east*. His voice was like the sound of many waters; and *the earth shone with His glory.*" (Ezekiel 43:1–2) If that is the pattern, then we can understand the following verse: "…The *Sun of Righteousness* shall arise *With healing in His wings…*" (Malachi 4:2)

The word *"Sun"* in the above verse is translated from the Hebrew word, *"Shemesh"* (שֶׁמֶשׁ), which means, *"Sun rising"* and interestingly, *"the East."* The Sun in this verse is symbolic of the *Brilliance of Righteousness* rising. It comes with healing in God's wings. The word *"wings"* is from the Hebrew word, *"Kanaph"* (כָּנָף), which is the same word for the *"tassles"* on the Tallit in Numbers 15:38 and is also mentioned in the following verse: "And He rode upon a cherub and flew; He flew upon the *wings of the wind.*" (Psalm 18:10)

As the wind has *"wings,"* it explains how God's voice would come walking in the *"…cool of the day…."* He would come as Light from the East riding on the wings of the *"wind of the day-light."* If Adam would choose the tree of life, then the *"Way of Righteousness"* would be open to all mankind. The tree of life, which would lead to *"Life"*! The *Sun* of righteousness would arise from the East of Eden into the Earth, with healing in his wings. "In the *way of righteousness is life*, And in its pathway, there is no death." (Proverbs 12:28)

However, if Adam chose the tree of the knowledge of good and evil, then the *"way of death"* would be opened to humanity and darkness coupled with the *shadow of death* would be overcast over humanity. *"There is a way that seems right to a man, But its end is the way of death."* (Proverbs 16:25)

God was confident that Adam would choose the tree of life *if he obeyed His Voice*. However, another voice wanted Adam to choose the tree of the knowledge of good and evil. This was the voice of the serpent. We are told in the following scripture, about the serpent's character: "Now the serpent was more *cunning* than any beast of the field which the Lord God had made." (Genesis 3:1) The word *"cunning"* above is from the Hebrew word "*Arum*" (עָרוּם), which means, *"crafty"* or *"shrewd."*

The serpent wanted Adam to disobey God's voice. Why? Because Adam would become bound in afflictions and irons. "Those who sat in darkness and in the shadow of death, Bound in affliction and irons. Because they *rebelled against the words of God*, And despised the counsel of the Most High," (Psalm 107:11) The comparison between the two trees was very simple to understand. However, "...the serpent deceived Eve by his craftiness...," so that her "...mind was corrupted from the simplicity..." of the tree of life and from understanding the danger the forbidden tree imparted.

We can see the progression of the serpent's craftiness: "And he said to the woman, "Has God indeed said, 'You shall not eat of *every tree of the garden*'?"" (Genesis 3:1) The serpent does *not* ask, "...*Has God indeed said, 'You shall not eat of the tree of the knowledge of good and evil in the midst of the garden?'"*, instead. he sneakily asks, "...*Has God indeed said, 'You shall not eat of every tree of the garden'?*." Of course, Eve knows they were allowed to eat of all the trees of the garden except one tree: "And the woman said to the serpent, "We may eat the fruit of the trees of the garden; *but of the fruit of the tree, which is in the midst of the garden*, God has said, 'You shall not eat it, *nor shall you touch it*, lest you die.'" (Genesis 3:2)

If you notice, somehow, Eve misses the fact that the tree of life was also amid the garden. Both trees were amid the garden. So, which tree was she talking about? Maybe Adam and Eve had been avoiding both trees amid the garden. The serpent takes advantage of Eve's naivety by directing her to the one tree, by falsely claiming they "...*will be like God by knowing both good and evil...*" and avoids mentioning the tree of life, which was the correct choice: "Then the serpent said to the woman, "You will not surely die. For God knows that in the day you eat of it your eyes will be opened, and you will be like God, knowing good and evil."" (Genesis 3:4–5)

The serpent made Eve focus entirely on the tree of the knowledge of good and evil and it is not noted that she even glanced at the tree of life to compare. Instead, her gaze was now on this one tree and her perception of this tree had now changed from a tree of death (as God has said, "...*in the day you eat of it you shall surely die...*"), to a tree supposedly "...*good for food,...pleasant to the eyes, and...desirable to make one wise....*" "So, when the woman *saw* that the tree was good for food, that it was pleasant to the eyes, and a tree desirable to make one wise, she took of its fruit and ate. She also gave to her husband with her, and he ate. Then the eyes of both of them were opened, and they knew that they were naked; and they sewed fig leaves together and made themselves coverings." (Genesis 3:6-7)

Eve heeded the voice of the serpent and was deceived. "And the Lord God said to the woman, "What is this you have done?" The woman said, *"The serpent deceived me*, and I ate.'"" (Genesis 3:13) The phrase *"deceived me"* is translated from the Hebrew phrase *"Hissiani"* (הִשִּׁיאַנִי), which comes from the Hebrew root word, *"Nasha"* (נָשָׁא). *Nasha* interestingly means, *"to lend on interest"* or to put it in my terms, to become a *"creditor."* So, the serpent's main aim was also to put Mankind in *"debt,"* and he would be the *"creditor."* No wonder we needed to be *"redeemed."*

Then Adam heeded the voice of his wife to disobey God. "Then to Adam He said, "Because you have *heeded the voice of your wife*, and have eaten from the tree of which I commanded you, saying, 'You shall not eat of it':" (Genesis 3:17)

The Adam Blueprint

Adam's participation in the serpent's cunning scheme was of the utmost importance. I want you to note that nothing affected Eve until she gave the fruit to Adam. After Adam ate, immediately it says, *"...Then the eye of both of them were opened..."* "...she took of its fruit and ate. She also gave to her husband with her, and he ate. Then the eyes of both of them were opened," (Genesis 3:6–7)

You must understand that the command was only given to Adam because he was alone and did not yet have Eve with him: "And the Lord God *commanded the man*, saying, "Of every tree of the garden you may freely eat; *but* of the *tree of the knowledge of good and evil you shall not eat*, for in the day that you eat of it you shall surely die.'"" (Genesis 2:16–17)

This can be explained when we understand that the name Adam was not a *descriptive* but a *"functional"* name. Most of the names given by God to men in the Bible were functional as opposed to being descriptive. As such, many times, the Hebrew word *"Adam"* (הָאָדָם) is translated descriptively as *"mankind"* or from its Hebrew root word, *"Adom"* (אָדָם), which means *"red,"* or *"blood"* often summarized that he was made from "red dust."

The Adam Principle

The English word for *"man"* in the above passage, in verse sixteen is the Hebrew word, *"Adam"* (הָאָדָם) instead of the Hebrew word, *"ish"* (אִישׁ), which is also translated as *"man"* in English sometimes. Throughout Genesis chapters one through Three, these two Hebrew names are used but they both carry a different *function*. But look carefully below: "But for Adam there was not found a helper comparable to him. And the Lord God caused a deep sleep to fall on Adam, and he slept; and He took one of his ribs and closed up the flesh in its place. Then *the rib* which the Lord God had taken from *man* (Adam-הָאָדָם) He made into a *woman* (Ishshah-נָשִׁים), and He brought her to the man (Adam-הָאָדָם)." (Genesis 2:20–22)

So, part of the above passage should read like this in English, "...*Then the rib which the LORD God had taken from Adam He made into a woman, and He brought her to Adam.*" I will explain in just a bit why this is significant. Let us review the scripture: "And *Adam said*: "This is now bone of my bones And flesh of my flesh; She shall be called Woman ("Ishshah"-נָשִׁים), Because she was taken out of Man ("ish" (אִישׁ). Therefore, a man ("ish" (אִישׁ) shall leave his father and mother and be joined to his wife ("Ishshah"-אִשָּׁה), and they shall become one("echad"-אֶחָד) flesh." (Genesis 2:20–22)

Read it this way: *"...the rib which the LORD God had taken from Adam He made into Ishshah...,"* then, *"...And Adam said...She shall be called Ishshah because she was taken out of Ish..."* To explain, notice that Adam was *created* in God's image and likeness. "So, God created man (Adam-הָאָדָם) in His own image; in the image of God, He created him; male and female He created them." (Genesis 1:27)

"This is the book of the genealogy of *Adam*. In the day that God created man (Adam-הָאָדָם), He made him in the likeness of God" (Genesis 5:1) Please note carefully, that there was a progression in Adam's manifestation. God first *created* Adam in Genesis 1:27, then afterward God *formed* Adam in Genesis 2:7. So, here is the order of Adam's and Eve's manifestation:

Step 1: *Adam is "created"*

God *created* Adam, in his image and likeness as noted below. The Hebrew word used in the verse below for the English word *"created"* is "Bara" (בָּרָא). At this stage, Adam was not yet formed and was not yet a *"living being"* on the earth. Notice also, that only Adam below is pointed out as being created *in the image of God*: I will explain. Then it says God created *"them"* male and female but not yet *"formed."*

"So, God created ("Bara"- בָּרָא) man (Adam-הָאָדָם) in His own image; in the image of God, He created ("Bara"- בָּרָא) *him*; male and female He created ("Bara"- בָּרָא) *them*. (Genesis 1:27)

Step 2: *Adam is "formed"*

God *"formed"* Adam out of the dust of the ground. The Hebrew word used in the verse below for the English word *"formed"* is *"Yatsar"* (יָצַר). As you can see below, the formation of Adam was in Genesis 2:7, not Genesis 1:27.

"And the Lord God formed ("Yatsar" - יָצַר) man (Adam-הָאָדָם) of the dust of the ground and breathed into his nostrils the breath of life; and man (Adam-הָאָדָם) became a living being." (Genesis 2:7)

The Hebrew word *"Yatsar"* is translated in other verses as a *"Potter, fashion, frame"* as in the verses below: "You shall break them with a rod of iron; You shall dash them to pieces like a *potter's* ("Yatsar" - יָצַר) vessel." (Psalm 2:9)

"Surely you have things turned around! Shall the *potter* ("Yatsar" - יָצַר) be esteemed as the clay; For shall the thing made say of him who made it, "He did not make me"? Or shall the thing *formed* ("Yetser"- יֵצֶר) say of him who *formed* ("Yatsar" - יָצַר) it, "He has no understanding"?" (Isaiah 29:16) As you can see from Isaiah 29:16, the word *"formed"* is connected to a *"Potter."* What does a Potter do with clay? So, picture God forming Adam out of the dust of the ground like a Potter forming an object out of clay.

Step 3: *Eve is taken out of Adam and "built"*

God took a rib out of Adam and then *built* Eve out of the rib. The English word *"made"* in the verse below is translated from the Hebrew word *"Banah" (בָּנָה)*, which means *"to build."*

"And the Lord God caused a deep sleep to fall on Adam, and he slept; and He took one of his ribs and closed up the flesh in its place. Then the rib which the Lord God had taken from man He *made* ("Banah"- בָּנָה) into a woman, and He brought her to the man." (Genesis 2:21–22)

Adam, the Glory of God.

As noted in step 2 of Adam's manifestation, Adam *came out of God*. Adam's essence came out of God's breath! "And the Lord God formed man (Adam-הָאָדָם) of the dust of the ground and breathed into his nostrils the breath of life; and man (Adam-הָאָדָם) became a living being." (Genesis 2:7)

Therefore, the essence of Adam was breathed *out of* God and had the *image* and *resemblance of* his glory. So, Adam had God's glory alone and there was none comparable to him. "…But for Adam there was not found a helper comparable to him." (Genesis 2:20)

The Hebrew word, *"ezer"* (עֵזֶר) means *"a helper"* and *"neged"* (נֶגֶד) means a *"part opposite"* or *"counterpart."* There was no *part opposite helper* found for Adam. Adam was looking. However, God had a better plan. Instead of searching the garden to find a helper for Adam, God took out of Adam a rib. From the rib *"…taken out of Adam…,"* God created a *"fully grown"* woman. God took what was of Adam's bone to *build* the woman. She was more than a part-opposite helper: she was *"…bone of my bone and flesh of my flesh…."* She was the *Glory of Adam* because she was created *out of Adam*:

"For a man indeed ought not to cover his head, since *he is the image and glory of God; but woman is the glory of man. For man is not from woman, but woman from man.*" (1 Corinthians 11:7–8)

Defining Adam

To fully understand Adam, we must look at his name. As the following verse says: "Whatever one is, *he has been named* already, *For it is known that he is man (Adam)*; And he cannot contend with Him who is mightier than he." (Ecclesiastes 6:10)

What is the function of Adam? his function is detailed in his name. The importance, significance and *function* of the name Adam can be seen in the Hebrew letters *"Aleph," "Dalet"* and *"Mem,"* which form up the name, Adam.

- Aleph (א) stands for "Strength or Leader,"
- Dalet (ד) stands for a "Tent Door or Pathway"
- Mem (מ) stands for "Water or Chaos."

Also, please note again that the two Hebrew words *Dalet* (ד) and *Mem* (מ) form the word *"Dam"* (דָם), which means *"Blood."* So, the function of the name Adam could be noted as a *"strong or leading door for the waters, blood or chaos"* coming from God, as God was Adam's source. Why strength or leadership?

God had given him *dominion* over creation on earth. Why Water or Blood? Because Water represents Life and blood has life in it (Leviticus: 17:11) and it has a voice (Genesis 4:10). It is interesting that Genesis 2:7, says God formed Adam out of the dust *"...of the ground...."* The Hebrew word for ground is *"Adamah"* (אֲדָמָה), which the Jewish Sages claim is *"red"* soil. Adam was made in the image of God, so he was a source of a *strong flow of living waters and blood.*

But Adam has another function of being *"Ish"* (man) so that he can become *"one flesh"* with *"Ishshah"* (woman) for the purposes of being fruitful to multiply. Why? So that God does not have to take another rib out of Adam's side. Instead, *"Ish"* could have relations with *"Ishshah"* and birth children through her womb. That is why Adam later calls *"Ishshah,"* a new name.

"And Adam called his wife's name Eve (Chavvah- חַוָּה), because she was the mother of all living." (Genesis 3:20)

This statement indicates that there was not going to be another man with the function of Adam from whom a rib would be taken out to create another comparable helper. But all offspring would come through the womb of a woman, so Adam *honored* her by naming her *Eve* or in Hebrew, *"Chavvah"* (חַוָּה), which means *"life-giver."* Interestingly, the Hebrew word for *"mother"* is *"Em"* (אֵם), which has the following letters:

- Aleph (א) stands for "Strength or Leader,"
- Mem (מ) stands for "Water or Chaos."

If you notice, the letter *"Dalet"* is missing. So, she was not the *"door."* Adam was the door! That explains why the Bible says the following: For Adam was formed first, then Eve." (1Timothy 2:13) And from Adam came every nation: "And He has made from one blood every nation of men to dwell on all the face of the earth, and has determined their preappointed times and the boundaries of their dwellings," (Acts 17:26) The word *'blood'* is missing from the original Greek text of the above verse, but the verse notes all nations of men came from *"one"* i.e., Adam, whose name is also described as *'blood.'*

So, knowing the difference between the Hebrew words "*Adam*" and "*Ish,*" the function of the name Adam was monumental when they ate from the tree of the knowledge of good and evil. Recall Adam's function was a *"strong door for the waters and blood."* As such, whatever came out of Adam directly affected the woman in equal measure as they were now *"one"* and he was the door. So, the strong waters coming out of Adam were imparted equally into the woman, enabling her to be a *comparable helper.*

The function of *"Adam"* explains why the commandment regarding the forbidden tree was only given to him. If he ate from that tree, he would be the door for good and evil to enter humanity: *Ishshah* first! *As he was, so she would be because she came out of him.* Eve would be the mother of all humanity with the contamination of good and evil. So, this explains why both of their *"...eyes were opened..."* only after Adam ate the fruit! Had Adam refused to eat the fruit even after the woman had eaten it, she would have been saved by his strong waters and blood cleansing her. However, when he ate the fruit of the Tree of the knowledge of good and evil, it became Adam's *source* and now he had become a *"strong door for chaos"* and this was translated to the woman as she was "one" with Adam. As they were one, whatever happened to Adam, happened to Eve.

This chaos contaminated their waters and their blood. From the moment Adam ate the fruit, Eve became contaminated so that whatever came out of Eve's womb would be *birthed in chaos* as their blood was now contaminated and its voice spoke condemnation and their waters flowed in the way of death. As the animals did not come out of Adam, their blood was not contaminated; that is why the *blood of animals* later continuously played a significant role in sacrifices, in the Law of Moses and all the way *until* John's Baptism *with water.*

"Therefore, not even the first covenant was dedicated without blood. For when Moses had spoken every precept to all the people according to the law, he took *the blood of calves and goats, with water,* scarlet wool, and hyssop, and sprinkled both the book itself and all the people, saying, "This is *the blood of the covenant* which God has commanded you."" (Hebrews 9:18–20)

I call the total effect Adam had on humanity, *the Adam Blueprint.* He alone became the *"doorway"* for chaos; sin and death to enter humanity. Here is the Adam Blueprint explained in the following verses: "Therefore, just as through one man sin entered the world, and death through sin, and thus death spread to all men, because all sinned—...Therefore, as through one man's offense judgment came to all men, resulting in condemnation, …For as by one man's disobedience many were made sinners, …" (Romans 5:12,18–19)

The above verses very specifically point out that it was *"…one man's…" action, offense, and disobedience* that caused the resulting sin, death, judgment and resulting in condemnation to enter *all* humanity. Because of Adam's disobedience, *all became sinners*. Had Adam eaten from the tree of life, he would have become a *Strong Door for the Waters of Life* but instead, he became a strong door for chaos. As Eve was affected having *"come out of"* Adam, she become the mother of all, with each person being born into chaos, having the seed of the knowledge of good and evil.

The Revelation of Mashiach And The Son of Man

If Adam alone could bring chaos into the world, which would affect *all mankind* to this day, then only *another* Adam, who is superior would be needed to reverse and erase where the first Adam failed. As such, the mystery of God's plan for redemption was to bring *another Adam*. This *second Adam* would be the *"Christ"* in Greek, *"Mashiach"* in Hebrew or *"Messiah"* in English, which all mean the *"Anointed One."* The knowledge of the *Mashiach* is that He would be a King, descended from the line of David that would usher in the Messianic age, which includes the building of the Temple in Jerusalem, world peace, and the unification of the Tribes of Israel in the world to come. I agree with this, however, God always had more for the *Mashiach*:

"Indeed, He says, 'It is too small a thing that You should be My Servant To raise up the tribes of Jacob, And to restore the preserved ones of Israel; I will also give You as a light to the Gentiles, That You should be My salvation to the ends of the earth.'" (Isaiah 49:6) As you can see, God had more than just raising up the tribes of Jacob and restoring the preserved ones of Israel. God also intended that the *Mashiach* would be a *"light to the gentiles"* and that He would be *"My Salvation"* to the ends of the earth. Interestingly, the Hebrew word for Salvation is *"Yeshua."*

The *mystery* of the *Mashiach* or Christ is that He is *the last Adam*. This mystery was hidden through the ages and has been revealed to the Gentiles through the revelation given to Paul as noted in the following verse: "To me, who am less than the least of all saints, this grace was given, that I should preach among the Gentiles the unsearchable riches of Christ, and to make all see what the fellowship of *the mystery*, which from the beginning of the ages has been hidden in God…" (Ephesians 3:8–9)

As you can see above, the *Mashiach* had more unsearchable riches than what was known about Him. "the mystery which has been hidden from ages and from generations, but now has been revealed to His saints. To them God willed to make known what are the riches of the glory of this mystery among the Gentiles: which is Christ in you, the hope of glory." (Colossians 1:26–27)

God intended to have the *Mashiach* to be *"in you"* before He would return as a King on the earth. "if indeed you have heard of the dispensation of the grace of God which was given to me for you, how that by revelation He made known to me the mystery (as I have briefly written already, by which, when you read, you may understand my knowledge in the mystery of Christ), which in other ages was not made known to the sons of men, as it has now been revealed by the Spirit to His holy apostles and prophets…" (Ephesians 3:2-5)

This mystery was hidden and was revealed to the gentiles who were not seeking the God of Abraham, Isaac, and Jacob but through the revelation of the mystery found Him. "I was sought by those who did not ask for Me; I was found by those who did not seek Me. I said, 'Here I am. Here I am,' To a nation that was not called by My Name." (Isaiah 65:1) Without the teachings of Christ, I would not have known about the God of the Hebrews. It is through the revealing of his mystery that I got to know the true God and to love Him and his word and to know and to love the nation of Israel and its people. Without Christ, I would not have known anything about God. I know this is true about many gentiles that love the Hebrew scriptures.

The *Mashiach*'s first role was to reverse the effects of the first Adam on all of humanity. "For as in Adam all die, even so in Christ all shall be made alive" (1 Corinthians 15:22) The verse compares the role of Adam versus the role of Christ (*Mashiach*). "And so, it is written, "The first man Adam became a living being." The last Adam became a life-giving Spirit." (1 Corinthians 15:45) This confirms that the *Mashiach (Christ) is the last Adam* as *"…in Adam all die, even so in Christ all shall be made alive….." There will only be two Adams that will ever be on the earth*; the first Adam who became a *living being* and the last Adam Who became a *life-giving Spirit*.

In Judaism, the *Mashiach* is a human, physically descended from King David, however, there is doubt if He would be the Son of God. So, if the last

Adam is Christ or *Mashiach*, is He divine? Yes! The first Adam was called a *"son of God"*: "the son of Methuselah, the son of Enoch, the son of Jared, the son of Mahalalel, the son of Cainan, the son of Enosh, the son of Seth, the son of *Adam, the son of God*." (Luke 3:37–38)

He was made in the image of God: "Then God said, "Let Us make man in *Our image*, according to *Our likeness*." (Genesis 1:26)

In the above verse, the word "man" is translated from *"Adam."* So, the correct phrase would be, *"...Let Us make Adam in Our image, according to Our likeness...."* So, it is not that all humanity was made in God's image, Adam was the one made in his image, therefore, Adam was called the *son of God*. Adam was the *"...the Image and Glory of God..."* "For a man indeed ought not to cover his head, since he is the image and glory of God." (1 Corinthians 11:7–8)

However, when Adam sinned, he fell. He fell from what? He fell from the Glory of God. And so, we who were born out of Adam *"...fell short of the Glory...."* "for *all* have sinned and *fall short of the glory of God*," (Romans 3:23)

If the first Adam was called the *son of God*, but fell short of the Glory, the last Adam must excel in all ways if He is a *life-giving Spirit*. That means He had to *come from Heaven*. That is why God was sorry that He had made the first Adam *"on the earth."* "And the LORD was sorry that He had made man on the earth, and He was grieved in His heart." (Genesis 6:6)

In the Hebrew, it is the phrase *"baares haadam"* (הָאָדָם בָּאָרֶץ), which is *"...Adam on the earth...."* The LORD was sorry for having *made Adam on the Earth*! So, God made sure the Last Adam had to *come from Heaven*: "The first man was of the earth, made of dust; the second Man is the Lord from Heaven" (1 Corinthians 15:47)

The English word *"man"* in the above verse is translated from the Greek word *"ánthrōpos,"* usually meant for *"mankind"* is different from the Greek word used for an individual man or male, which is *"anḗr."* According to Strong's concordance, *"...ánthrōpos ("man") answers to the Hebrew term, 'adam - and 435 (anḗr) answers to the Hebrew term 'ish."* So, the previous verse (1 Corinthians 15:47) can be read as,

"...The first Adam was of the earth, made of dust; the second Adam is the Lord from Heaven...."

This Greek word *Anthropos* is used in many verses in the New Testament and is translated simply as *"man"* or *"men"* as in the following verse:

"Then He said to them, "Follow Me, and I will make you fishers of men (Anthropos)." (Matthew 4:19)

However, in some instances, especially when Yeshua uses the word when He calls Himself the *"Son of Man"* (*huios tou anthropos*), it has to do more with *anthropos* in terms of *"mankind"* concerning one man. i.e., *mankind coming out of one man*. As Strong's noted, *"…ánthrōpos ("man") answers to the Hebrew term, 'adam."* Concerning Yeshua, the term *"son of anthropos"* was in answer *to Adam*. As Anthropos is defined simply as mankind, concerning Yeshua, Anthropos means *a single being with the ability to host all mankind inside of Himself.*

"When Jesus came into the region of Caesarea Philippi, He asked His disciples, saying, "Who do men say that I, the Son (huios) of Man (ánthrōpos), am?" So, they said, "Some say John the Baptist, some Elijah, and others Jeremiah or one of the prophets." He said to them, "But who do you say that I am?" Simon Peter answered and said, "You are the Christ, the Son of the living God." Jesus answered and said to him, "Blessed are you, Simon Bar-Jonah, for flesh and blood has not revealed this to you, but My Father who is in heaven. (Matthew 16:13–17)

The Greek word for *"son"* here is *"Huios,"* which according to Strong's Concordance means, *"anyone sharing the same nature as their father."* So, the phrase *"son of man"* about *Yeshua* or *"huios tou anthropos"* would mean the *"one sharing the same nature as Adam."* When saying *the same nature as Adam*, I mean the same impact on all humanity from one person as Adam solely had on us.

Otherwise, if Yeshua meant the term *"son of man"* when referencing Himself as simply a "son of a human," then we would have to explain a few scriptures as such these:

"But that you may know that the Son of Man has power on earth to forgive sins"—then He said to the paralytic, "Arise, take up your bed, and go to your house." (Matthew 9:6)

"For the Son of Man is Lord even of the Sabbath." (Matthew 12:8)

"For the Son of Man has come to save that which was lost." (Matthew 18:11)

"The Son of Man will send out His angels, and they will gather out of His kingdom all things that offend, and those who practice lawlessness," (Matthew 13:41)

"just as the Son of Man did not come to be served, but to serve, and to give His life a ransom for many." (Matthew 20:28)

So, in Matthew 16, Simon Peter got the revelation from Heaven that Yeshua Who called Himself *"huios tou anthropos (Son of Man)* was *"...the Christ, the Son of the Living God..."*

We know this verse and we know that Peter got the revelation about Yeshua being the Christ (*Mashiach*). However, Yeshua had an additional revelation for them. Yeshua did not ask if men say He is the Christ! Let us phrase it this way as in the Greek text: *"Who do anthropos say that I, huios tou Anthropos, am?."* The same word is used twice! However, I think what he meant to say was, *"Who do men say that I, the one sharing the same nature as Adam, am?"* He wanted to know if they knew if He was the *last Adam*! After inquiring about what other men say, He then asked them, *"But who do you say that I am?."*

The revelation Peter got from the Father in Heaven was two-fold with one clear and one hidden: Yeshua is the *Mashiach* (Christ), the Messenger Who is sent by God from heaven. Yeshua, the one sharing the same nature as *Adam* is the son of the living God!

Paul revealed the mystery of Yeshua as being the last Adam: "And so it is written, "The first man Adam became a living being." The last Adam became a life-giving spirit." (1 Corinthians 15:45) On the *Rock* of Yeshua, being *the last Adam* and *the Christ*, He would build his congregation. The Jewish people through Moses had always known the Prophet or *Mashiach* would come to redeem them. What they did not know or what was not fully revealed was that He would also come as the *"Last Adam"* through Whom *all humanity* would be hosted in Him so that all humanity could be redeemed through Him.

So, the *Mashiach* was not only coming to save the Jewish people from their oppressors or to give us Salvation so that we escape eternal damnation. Christ was to come as the last Adam to take humanity to a whole new level in God. The first Adam was a son of God from the Earth. The last Adam was the Son of God from heaven. "The first man was of the earth, made of dust; the second Man is the Lord from Heaven" (1 Corinthians 15:47)

Why is this particularly important? Because of the following as explained by Paul: "However, the spiritual is not first, but the natural, and afterward the spiritual." (1 Corinthians 15:46) So, for our benefit He was a Heavenly Man: "As was the man of dust, so also are those who are made of dust; and as is the heavenly Man, so also are those who are heavenly. And as we have borne the image of the man of dust, we shall also bear the image of the heavenly Man." (1 Corinthians 15:48–49)

Because He is Adam, we can live *"in"* Him. In Him are all dimensions. The first Adam ate from the tree of the knowledge of good and evil. The last Adam is life itself. "Jesus said to him, I am the way, the truth, and the Life…" (John 14:6)

The first Adam brought sin and death: "Therefore, just as through *one man* sin entered the world, and death through sin, and thus *death spread to all men*," (Romans 5:12)

The last Adam brought life: "…I have come that they may have Life, and that they may have it more abundantly" (John 10:10) The law of sin and death was set due to the first Adam, but the last Adam set humanity free through the law of the Spirit of Life: " For the law of the Spirit of Life in Christ Jesus has made me free from the law of sin and death." (Romans 8:2)

Just like the first enemy Adam brought to humanity was *death*, death will be the last enemy to be destroyed. "The last enemy that will be destroyed is death" (1 Corinthians 15:26)

It is truth when it is said, *"So the last will be first, and the first last."* So, the last Adam shall be first and the first Adam last.

God's Spectacular Reconciliation Through the Last Adam

How did He accomplish this? God breathed into Adam. As He breathed into Adam, He also released all of *mankind* into Adam. So, Adam was carrying all of mankind inside of him. Mankind was 'one' with Adam. That is why when he saw Eve, he said, she was *"…bone of my bone, flesh of my flesh…" (Genesis 2:23)*, not that she resembled him or looked like him as a human, but because she came out of him. Hence why he called her woman, meaning *out of man*. I should emphasize that the scriptures already show that no matter how distant the people that came out of Adam were, whatever Adam was spiritually, they became. As he was, so they became.

When Adam was kicked out of the garden, we were all kicked out! So, this was the *blueprint* of the living being called *Adam*. No other man on the earth was created like Adam or had such an impact on mankind. However, God's amazing plan was hidden from the time Adam fell. He planned to bring *another Adam* as mentioned in the last chapter to redeem mankind from what the first Adam did. This is how it happened.

Most of the world knows that saints (believers in Christ) believe that Jesus (Yeshua) is the Christ Who died for their sins on the cross. He is known as the *"lamb of God who takes away the sin of the world"* as John says in *John 1:29*. If Yeshua is the *Mashiach* or Christ, then He is the *"Last Adam."* We can only know this by seeing how He functioned as an Adam. So, how did He accomplish the role of being the last Adam?

By following the *blueprint of Adam*, which had to do with mankind. Let me explain. When Yeshua was put on the cross, He took on the condemnation and the punishment that was deserved by all of *mankind* because of the sin of the first Adam. "Therefore, as through one man's offense judgment came to all men, resulting in condemnation" (Romans 5:18)

He went to the Cross as Adam because only *an* Adam or *"anthropos"* could represent all *mankind*. Through the first Adam, we had all become sinners because he represented all mankind. "Therefore, just as *through one-man* sin entered the world, and death through sin, and thus death spread to all men, because all sinned- (For until the law sin was in the world, but sin is not imputed when there is no law.") (Romans 5:12-13)

All mankind whether born or not yet born were all sinners because as the first Adam was, so was all mankind. And because of the law of Moses, sin was now *imputed* into man as noted in *verse thirteen* above. For the law of Moses made all *guilty* or accountable before God. "Now we know that whatever the law says, it says to those who are under the law, that every mouth may be stopped, and all the world may become guilty before God." (Romans 3:19)

So, mankind was not only sinning but had become sin, itself and had all but become guilty before God. So, for God to redeem mankind, HE had to use the Adam blueprint, otherwise all of mankind would *individually* have to sacrifice animals to have their sins atoned. So, when Yeshua was at the cross, He *took into Himself* all sinful mankind. When I say *all*, I mean *all* of mankind: every human being from the time of Adam and beyond the time when you are reading this book, until the end of time. Even you who are reading this: Yeshua took you into Himself. Why? Because He was the Last Adam, the *last Anthropos* who came to redeem all mankind.

Many Jewish people had looked up to Yeshua to be King as they expected the *Mashiach* to be king over them and save them from their enemies. "Therefore, when Jesus perceived that they were about to come and take Him by force to make Him king, He departed again to the mountain by Himself alone." (John 6:15) But at the time, they did not know the plan of God for the redemption of the world first. So, as they were disappointed that Yeshua was on the cross, He was following the Adam *blueprint of God*

The Adam Principle

(the first Adam had all of mankind in himself), by taking all of mankind *into* Himself at the Cross.

I always thought that only my sin was with Him at the cross. I did not realize until God gave me the revelation that I was on that cross as well, *in* Yeshua! You were on that cross with Him. He took you in without you knowing it. All of humanity was with Him on the Cross! When He took us into Himself, He took on all our sins, like a lamb sacrificed to atone for the sin of a nation. Instead of all of mankind being wiped out as the punishment of sin was death, He as Adam, took on our punishment.

"Surely He has borne our griefs And carried our sorrows; Yet we esteemed Him stricken, Smitten by God, and afflicted. But He was wounded for our transgressions, He was bruised for our iniquities; The chastisement for our peace was upon Him, And by His stripes we are healed. All we like sheep have gone astray; We have turned, everyone, to his own way; And the Lord has laid on Him the iniquity *of us all*. He was oppressed, and He was afflicted, Yet He opened not His mouth; He was led as a lamb to the slaughter, And as a sheep before its shearers is silent. So, He opened not His mouth. He was taken from prison and from judgment, And who will declare His generation? For He was cut off from the land of the living; For the transgressions of My people, He was stricken. And they made His grave with the wicked— But with the rich at His death because He had done no violence, Nor was any deceit in His mouth. Yet it pleased the Lord to bruise Him; He has put Him to grief. When You make His soul an offering for sin, He shall see His seed, He shall prolong His days, And the pleasure of the Lord shall prosper in His hand. He shall see the labor of His soul and be satisfied. By His knowledge, My righteous Servant shall justify many, For He shall bear their iniquities. Therefore, I will divide Him a portion with the great, And He shall divide the spoil with the strong, Because He poured out His soul unto death, And He was numbered with the transgressors, And *He bore the sin of many,* And made intercession for the transgressors." (Isaiah 53:4–12)

So, now it makes sense when it says, *"...Yet is pleased the LORD to bruise Him...."* Why? Because He was an Adam. The result of this would affect *all* mankind. God knew this and that is why it says in *verse eleven*, *"...My righteous Servant shall justify many, For He shall bear their iniquities..."*

However, here is the incredible part. As He had absorbed us in Himself at the cross, *when He died, we died with Him!* "...what you sow is not made alive unless it dies. And what you sow, you do not sow that body that shall be, but mere grains-perhaps wheat or some other grain. But God gives it a body as He pleases, and to each seed its own body." (1 Corinthians 5:37–38)

As the first Adam was, so was everyone that came out of him. So as Yeshua was, so was everything that came into Him and out of Him; that is the *Adam blueprint of God*. So, when He died to sin, we also died to sin at that instant.

"What shall we say then? Shall we continue in sin that grace may abound? Certainly not! How shall *we who died* to sin live any longer in it? Or do you not know that *as many of us as were baptized into Christ Jesus were baptized into His death?*" (Romans 6:1–3)

"For he who has died has been freed from sin. *Now if we died with Christ*, we believe that we shall also live with Him," (Romans 6:7–8) "This is a faithful saying: For if we died with Him, we shall also live with Him." (2 Timothy 2:11) The death of Yeshua was certainly not just for your sins. His death on the cross included you! You died inside of Him and were buried inside of Him. When He was buried, we were also buried. "Therefore, *we were buried with Him* through baptism into death," (Romans 6:4)

So, notice it says we were *buried* with Him "*...through baptism....*" When was this baptism? It was during the baptism of John that Yeshua (as Adam) absorbed us into his death. As He immersed into the river waters, He absorbed all that were *baptized*. That is why new believers get baptized in water. When He came out of the water, He was baptized in the Spirit. So, when we come out of the water, we can pray to be baptized in the Spirit as well.

In his death, You were part of the process because when '*an Adam*' is involved, it always affects all of humanity. He included you! Why? It was to create something new. How? "*...that just as Christ was raised from the dead by the glory of the Father, even so we also should walk in newness of life. For if we have been united together in the likeness of His death*, certainly we also shall be in the likeness of His resurrection, knowing this, *that our old man was crucified with Him*, that the body of sin might be done away with, that we should no longer be slaves of sin. For he who has died has been freed from sin. *Now if we died with Christ,* we believe that we shall also live with Him, *knowing that Christ, having been raised from the dead*, dies no more. Death no longer has dominion over Him. For the death that He died, He died to sin once for all; but the life that He lives, He lives to God. Likewise, you also, *reckon yourselves* to *be dead indeed to sin*, but *alive to God* in Christ Jesus our Lord." (Romans 6:4–11)

And when he resurrected, we also resurrected to a new life! "For since by man came death, by Man also came the resurrection of the dead. For as in Adam all die, even so in Christ all shall be made alive." (1 Corinthians 15:21–22)

Praise GOD! The *Mashiach* was not only one who dies for our sins but was the Last Adam who absorbed us into Himself so that we can die with Him and die to sin and then resurrect with Him, so that death no longer has dominion over us. We are now made alive in Him!

Out of His Side, You Came forth

When God created Eve, it gives the following account, which you are familiar with: "And the LORD God caused a deep sleep to fall on Adam, and he slept; and He took one of his ribs and closed up the flesh in its place. Then *the rib* which the LORD God had taken from man He made into a woman, and He brought her to the man." (Genesis 2:21–22)

The English word *"rib"* is translated from the Hebrew word *"tsela"* (צֵלָע), which is also means *"side."* As you can see the same Hebrew word is used in the following passage: "And you shall make bars of acacia wood: five for the boards on *one side* (tsela) of the tabernacle, five bars for the boards on the *other side* (tsela) of the tabernacle…." (Exodus 26:26–27)

When Yeshua was at the Cross, it says he was pierced at his "side." "But one of the soldiers pierced His side with a spear, and immediately blood and water came out…" (John 19:34) When the soldier pierced his side, blood and water came out. Recall when I mentioned that *"…the function of the name Adam could be noted as a "strong or leading door for the waters, blood or chaos" coming from God? Why Water or Blood? Because Water represents Life and blood has life in it (Leviticus: 17:11) and it has a voice (Genesis 4:10) …."* I also mentioned earlier, *"…Adam was made in the image of God, so he was a source of a strong flow of living waters and blood…"*

As Yeshua had taken us *into Himself* and we died with Him on the Cross, He let us all *flow out of Him* through the gushing water and blood! We all came out of his side through the water and the blood! Why? His water washed you: "let us draw near with a true heart in full assurance of faith, having our hearts sprinkled from an evil conscience and *our bodies washed with pure water.*" (Hebrews 10:22)

Without Blood, there is no forgiveness: "And according to the law almost all things *are purified (cleansed) with blood,* and *without shedding of blood there is no remission (forgiveness).*" (Hebrews 9:22)

Therefore, coming out of Him through his blood, it washed and cleansed you from all sin: "But if we walk in the light as He is in the light, we have fellowship with one another, and the blood of Jesus Christ His Son cleanses us from all sin." (1 John 1:7) "…To Him Who loved us and *washed us from our sins in His own blood,* …" (Revelation 1:5)

His blood redeemed you: "knowing that you were not redeemed with corruptible things, like silver or gold, from your aimless conduct received by tradition from your fathers, *but with the precious blood of Christ,* as of a lamb without blemish and without spot." (1 Peter 1:18–19) "He has delivered us from the power of darkness and conveyed us into the kingdom of His Son of His love, in whom *we have redemption through His blood, the forgives of sins.*" (Colossians 1:13–14)

"*In Him we have redemption through His blood, the forgiveness of sins*, according to the riches of His grace." (Ephesians 1:7) This redemption includes you no matter your race, color, nationality, language: you are *all* included: "…For You were slain And have redeemed us to God by Your Blood out of *every tribe and tongue and people and nation,*" (Revelation 5:9) His blood justified you. i.e., made you righteous: "Much more then, *having now been justified by His blood*, we shall be saved from wrath through Him." (Romans 5:9)

His blood cleansed your conscience from dead works so you can properly serve God: "how much more shall the blood of Christ, Who through the Eternal Spirit offered Himself without spot to God, *cleanse your conscience from dead works to serve the living God*?" (Hebrews 9:14) His blood brought you into an everlasting Covenant with God:

"…He broke it and said, "Take, eat; this is My body which is broken for you; do this in remembrance of Me." In the same manner He also took the cup after supper, saying, "*This cup is the New Covenant in My Blood. This do, as often as you drink it, in remembrance of Me.*" (1 Corinthians 11:24–25) Why "*…in remembrance of Me…*"? because you went into Him and came out of Him through his blood. Remember, it is Him through Whom you were cleansed and brought into the Covenant. "Of How much worse punishment, do you suppose, will he be thought worthy who has trampled the Son of God underfoot, counted *the blood of the Covenant* by which he was sanctified a common thing, and insulted the Spirit of Grace?" (Hebrews 10:29)

His blood started to speak better things about you than the blood of Abel, which rightfully condemned Cain: "But you have come to Mount Zion and to the city of the living God, the heavenly Jerusalem, to an innumerable company of angels, to the general assembly and the church of the firstborn who are registered in heaven, to God the Judge of all, to the spirits of just men made perfect, to Jesus the Mediator of the New Covenant, and to *the blood* of sprinkling that speaks better things than that of Abel." (Hebrews 12:22–24)

His blood gave you access to the Holiest place: "Therefore, brethren, having boldness to *enter the Holiest by the blood of Jesus,*" (Hebrews 10:19) His blood brought you into peace with God: "For it pleased the Father that in Him all fullness should dwell, and by Him to reconcile all things to Himself, by Him, whether things on earth or things in heaven, *having made peace through the blood of His Cross.*" (Colossians 1:19–20) His blood brought you closer to God: "But now in Christ Jesus you who were once far off have been brought near by the blood of Christ." (Ephesians 2:13)

Yeshua, being the Last Adam, i.e., *John identifies the door of waters and blood*: "This is He Who came *by Water and Blood*-Jesus Christ; *not only by water, but by water and blood.* And it is the Spirit Who bears witness because the Spirit is Truth." (1 John 5:6)

It is that water and blood that came out of his *"side"* that testifies of Him being the Last Adam. As the last Adam, He was able to redeem all of humanity, including you by pushing you out of Himself through his side (just like Eve was brought out of Adam's side) in the water and the blood. As you know, nothing is established except *"...by the mouth of two or three witnesses..." (Deuteronomy 19:15 and 2 Corinthians 13:1)*.

"For there are three that bear witness in heaven: The Father, the Word, and the Holy Spirit; and these three are one. And there are three that bear witness on the earth: *the Spirit, the Water, and the Blood*; and these three agree as one." (1 John 5:7–8) He bore witness *on the Earth* with the pouring of the water and the blood coming out of his side. This was God's witness. "If we receive the witness of men, the witness of God is greater; for *this is the witness of God* which He has testified of His Son." (1 John 5:9)

For the first Adam, God took a rib from him. A rib is a bone. That is why Adam said, *"...This is now bone of my bones...."* (Genesis 2:23). However, with the last Adam, out of his side came water and blood and this time it is God testifying that the water and blood are part of Him. Yeshua took us in Himself and let us out through his side through the water and the blood and the Spirit of Truth bears' witness. If you are washed by the water and cleansed by the blood of Yeshua, the Spirit of Truth will bear witness that you are clean! How the Cross of Yeshua looked so meek and yet so powerful. "For the message of the Cross is foolishness to those who are perishing, but to us who are being saved *it is the power of God*" (1 Corinthians 1:18)

Understanding Being Born Again

As *'Anthropos'* is defined as mankind; it means Anthropos as a single being can *host all mankind inside of Himself.* As we saw in the last chapter, Yeshua did this at the cross. He took us all within Himself, died, resurrected, and let us out again. If you can picture this, it is like we died and were *"born again."*

Yeshua tried to explain this concept to a Jewish Ruler the name of Nicodemus: "There was a man of the Pharisees named Nicodemus, a ruler of the Jews. This man came to Jesus by night and said to Him, "Rabbi, we know that You are a teacher come from God; for no one can do these signs that You do unless God is with him." Jesus answered and said to him, "Most assuredly, I say to you, unless one is born again, he cannot see the kingdom of God." Nicodemus said to Him, "How can a man be born when he is old? Can he enter a second time into his mother's womb and be born?" (John 3:1–4)

The word *"again"* in the phrase *"born again"* is the Greek word *"anóthen"* (ἄνωθεν), which is literally *"from above."* Yeshua was saying to be *"born from above."* The phrase *'born again'* may have come from Nicodemus' question where he asks, *"Can he enter a second time into his mother's womb and be born?"* This is amazing because Yeshua tried to explain the function of the Last Adam to Nicodemus. Remember, the first Adam was a man of the earth, made of dust. "The first man was of the earth, made of dust; the second Man is the Lord from Heaven" (1 Corinthians 15:47)

Yeshua was telling Nicodemus, that for us to see the Kingdom of God, we must be born *from above*, meaning *born from Heaven*. How was this possible? Would God take us all to Heaven and then bring us down again? Or was God going to send us to Heaven and send us back into our mothers' wombs? Nicodemus did not understand Yeshua was talking about another Adam and that is why he asked, *"…How can a man be born when he is old? Can he enter a second time into his mother's womb and be born?"* What Yeshua was hinting at was God would use the Last Adam as the conduit to birth humanity again. However, this time, this Adam had to be *"from Heaven."* So, as you see above, *"...the second Man is the Lord from Heaven."*

Yeshua tries to explain more that this Adam is born of the Spirit: "Jesus answered, "Most assuredly, I say to you, unless one is born of water and the Spirit, he cannot enter the kingdom of God. That which is born of the flesh is flesh, and that which is born of the Spirit is Spirit." (John 3:5–6) Yeshua went deeper. He said we must be born of *water* and the *Spirit* (*not of the earth and dust*) to enter the Kingdom of God.

As the last Adam, if you recall, Yeshua was baptized in water by John and the Spirit of God came upon Him. So as the last Adam, He had become one born of water and the Spirit. The first Adam was born of the flesh, the second Adam is born of the Spirit. So, what comes out of the first Adam is flesh and what comes out of the second Adam is Spirit. "The wind blows where it wishes, and you hear the sound of it, but cannot tell where it comes from and where it goes. So is everyone who is born of the Spirit." (John 3:8)

Yeshua was saying, those *born of the Spirit* are different. So, Nicodemus not understanding the *function* of Adam asks: "Nicodemus answered and said to Him, "How can these things be?" (John 3:9) As a Ruler, Nicodemus was the most influential teacher in Israel and Yeshua expected him to know this as one who teaches the Torah and was expecting the *Mashiach*. "Jesus answered and said to him, "Are you the teacher of Israel, and you do not know these things?" (John 3:10)

Yeshua was telling Him what He knows and what He has seen concerning this matter: "Most assuredly, I say to you, We speak what We know and testify what We have seen, and you do not receive Our witness. If I have told you earthly things and you do not believe, how will you believe if I tell you heavenly things?" (John 3:11–12)

If Yeshua explained to us all about the first Adam, which concerned earthly things, and we did not believe, how would we believe about the last Adam, which concerned heavenly things? John the Immerser explained this: "He who comes from above is above all; he who is of the earth is earthly and speaks of the earth. He who comes from heaven is above all. And what He has seen and heard, that He testifies; and no one receives His testimony. He who has received His testimony has certified that God is true." (John 3:31–33)

The last Adam being from heaven would be as *"...He who comes from heaven is above all..."* Recall the phrase *'Son of Man,'* references *'Anthropos,'* or the Last Adam for Yeshua explains to Nicodemus where the Last Adam comes from: "No one has ascended to heaven but He Who *came down from Heaven,* that is *the Son of Man* Who is in Heaven." (John 3:13)

Then Yeshua reveals the *function* of the Last Adam and how humanity was going to be drawn to Him: "And as Moses lifted up the serpent in the wilderness, even so *the Son of Man be lifted up,* that whoever believed in Him should not perish but have eternal life." (John 3:14-15) The Last Adam would be lifted on a pole (cross) just like the serpent as Moses did: "Then the LORD said to Moses, "Make a fiery serpent, and set it on a pole; and it shall be that everyone who is bitten, when he looks at it, shall live." So, Moses made a bronze serpent, and put it on the pole; and so, it was, if a serpent had bitten anyone, when he looked at the bronze serpent, he lived." (Numbers 21:8–9)

For all bitten by the serpent, the venom was active or working until they saw the *sign* of a dead snake on a pole. So, the venom in them died because they saw the dead serpent lifted on a pole. This was not just for one moment for it says, *"...if a serpent had bitten anyone..."* That means *they believed* that this worked. So whenever one was bitten, they knew that if they looked at this bronze serpent on the pole, they would live. Humanity had been bitten by a serpent with the sting of death. God was going to put the serpent on a pole and when we see the death of its work, we would live.

So, the *'Son of Man'* being the *Son of God,* was sent because of God's love to accomplish the task of giving us everlasting life: "And as Moses lifted up the serpent in the wilderness, even so *the Son of Man be lifted up,* that whoever believed in Him should not perish but have eternal life. For God so loved the world that He gave His only begotten Son, that whoever believes in Him should not perish but have everlasting life." (John 3:14-16) The last Adam was not sent on a mission to just rescue a nation or to destroy the world. He came to save the World first. "For God did not send His Son into the world to condemn the world, but the world through Him might be saved." (John 3:17)

What Nicodemus grasped from this conversation was beyond what he had expected: humanity had to become born from above to see and enter the Kingdom of God only through the Son of Man being lifted and those who believe in Him receiving everlasting life. This was a much bigger plan than only rescuing the Jewish nation from its enemies and setting up a Kingdom. The *Mashiach* was to save the world first. He would come back a second time to save Israel and his people in the end and set up his Kingdom. Yeshua concludes: "He who believes in Him is not condemned; but he who does not believe is condemned already, because he has not believed in the name of the only begotten Son of God. And this is the condemnation, that the light has come into the world, and men loved darkness rather than light, because their deeds were evil. For everyone practicing evil hates the light and does not come to the light, lest his deeds should be exposed. But he who does the truth comes to the light, that his deeds may be clearly seen, that they have been done in God." (John 3:17–21)

"Love has been perfected among us in this: that we may have boldness in the day of judgement; because as He is, so are we in this world." (1 John 4:17) Only with Adam can you *be as He is*. As Yeshua is the Last Adam, He came to do away with the first Adam. God's ultimate plan, which was a mystery from the beginning was through the last Adam, He would reset humanity. When Yeshua resurrected, He pushed us out again, this time as a new creation as noted below: "Therefore, if anyone is in Christ, he is a new creation; old things have passed away; behold, all things have become new. (2 Corinthians 5:17)

God planned to start a new creation through a different Adam! The last Adam was the *Mashiach*, the Christ! So, as you read this today, all humanity is either under the first Adam or the second Adam: one brings death and the other brings life. Those under the first Adam are under the law of sin and death while those under the Last Adam are under the Law of the Spirit of life. "For the law of the Spirit of Life in Christ Jesus has made me free from the law of sin and death." (Romans 8:2)

This goes beyond circumcision: "For in Christ Jesus neither circumcision nor uncircumcision avails anything, but a new creation." (Galatians 6:15) In the Beginning, God started with the Heavens and Adam was the last of his creations because Adam was made from the dust of the earth. This time, He chose to start with the last Adam *coming from Heaven*, redeeming man, starting a new creation, defeating all God's enemies including death, then ending with new heavens and a new earth. "For behold, I create new heavens and a new earth; And the former shall not be remembered or come to mind." (Isaiah 65:17)

The last Adam was from Heaven, "For the bread of God is He Who comes down from heaven and gives life to the world." (John 6:33) What confused many at the time is that they expected a physical man to come and bring a physical, political kingdom to the earth. What was not understood was the magnitude of God's plan to bring redemption to all of humanity first. This could only be done by God, who sent his Son from heaven to accomplish what no man, even a prophet like Moses, an anointed king like king David, a man with wisdom like Solomon or a man with power like Elijah could achieve. No man on the earth could do what was done at the cross! No religion on the earth has such a supernatural event as the death and resurrection of Yeshua because all mankind was in it!

Yeshua told them but they could not understand at the time as it was a mystery hidden in God. "For the message of the cross is foolishness to those who are perishing, but to us who are being save it is the power of God." (1 Corinthians 1:18) The message of the cross is foolishness only if one does not understand it. Even I was naïve and could not comprehend the spectacular extent to which God was going to redeem man through his Adam blueprint.

Yeshua kept hinting at this: "I am the living bread which came down from heaven. If anyone eats of this bread, he will live forever; and the bread that I shall give is My flesh, which I shall give for the life of the world." (John 6:51) When He was talking about bread, He was talking *"Adam language."* He was talking about *where you will end up* if you eat this bread. The first Adam was told the *"bread"* he would eat, he would eat *till* he would return to the ground because he is *dust*. "In the sweat of your face you shall eat bread till you return to the ground, For out of it you were taken; For dust you are, and to dust you shall return." (Genesis 3:19) But it was not just for him individually, but for all mankind. All mankind would work for this bread and return *"...to the ground for out of it you were taken..."*

The bread Yeshua was talking about was *from Heaven* and if you ate it, you would *live forever*. "This is the bread which came down from heaven- not as your fathers ate the manna and are dead. He who eats this bread will live forever." (John 6:58) This living bread was for mankind. God's plan was for man to live forever but with the *bread that comes from heaven*, not with the *bread that comes from the sweat of man's face*. Mankind thrives from the bread that comes from the sweat on man's face. You are celebrated for *"sweat equity"* as they say. Yet, Yeshua says:

"But He answered and said, "It is written, 'Man shall not live by bread alone, but by every word that proceeds from the mouth of God.'" (Matthew 4:4) Here He is talking about the bread that comes from man's sweat i.e., man's labor. That bread from your sweat that the first Adam brought returns mankind to dust. So, there must be more to sustain mankind than sweat: every word that proceeds from the mouth of God.

Now God has given every man a choice; either choose the first Adam who will be last or choose the Last Adam Who will be First. The first Adam was told if he ate from the tree, death will be the result. The Last Adam was told He would be God's Salvation to all the peoples. Those who reject the Last Adam will be judged according to the law of Moses, that is why it says they will be "*...judged according to their works....*" Those who accept the last Adam will be judged according to the law of the Spirit of Life for their names will be "*...written in the Book of Life...,*" having received life from the Last Adam, *Yeshua HaMashiach.*

Chapter 5

The Trees in the Garden

Tree of Life Versus Tree of Knowledge

God had intended for Adam and Eve to primarily live from the Spirit of life within not from the knowledge of good and evil. With the Spirit of life within, the *Light of Life* was the most intimate way Adam and Eve would relate to God as He is Spirit, light, and life! God intended to become one with Adam through a *three-fold cord*. This is a pattern! "Though one may be overpowered by another, two can withstand him. And *a threefold cord is not quickly broken*." (Ecclesiastes 4:12)

So, if Adam and Eve had eaten from the tree of life, they would have a threefold cord with God in the following manner:

1. His image
2. His likeness
3. His life.

As you can see above, they would have had a much stronger bond with God. The life from the tree of life was not just a *"breath of life,"* it was Life itself! By eating from the tree of life, Adam would have transitioned from being a *"living being,"* who is dependent upon the *"breath of life"* to becoming one with Life. Adam would become a life-giver like God. However, through disobedience to God's instruction, below is a threefold cord, which resulted from eating from the tree of the knowledge of good and evil: his image, his likeness, *The* knowledge of good and evil.

Compare the following threefold cords:

The Trees in the Garden

God's Intention for Man	Result of Adam's Decision
1. His image	1. His image
2. His likeness	2. His likeness
3. His life	3. *The* knowledge of good and evil

Do you see an erroneous pattern in the *threefold cord* created by Adam's decision? Do you see why God did not want them eating from that tree? It would result in man being wrapped in carnal *knowledge instead of Life*! So, from this decision, man would be sustained by the *"breath of life"* instead of having life *within* himself and becoming *a life-giver*. Therefore, the fading of the breath of life would lead to aging and the eventual ceasing of this breath would lead to death, as God had warned.

When man stops breathing, the body ceases to function as the breath of life in the blood stops circulating. In addition, the knowledge of both good and evil and the operation of it would lead to sin. So, living by the breath and the operation of good and evil put man under a law: *the law of Sin and Death*.

Now that Adam chose the tree of knowledge of good and evil, he was going to relate to God *through knowledge*. God had intended for mankind to know Him *through Life*: "And *this is* Eternal Life, *that they may know You, the only true God, and Jesus Christ Whom You have sent*." (John 17:3)

Recall, Eve looked at the tree and saw this: "So when the woman saw that the tree was good for food, that it was pleasant to the eyes, and a tree desirable to *make one wise (lehaskil)*, she took of its fruit and ate." (Genesis 3:6) The phrase, "...*make one wise*..." is translated from the Hebrew word *"Lehaskil"* (לְהַשְׂכִּיל), which means to *"study, to learn, to succeed."* The word *"lehaskil"* comes from the Hebrew root word, *"sakal,"* which means *"intelligence, intellect and reason."* In other words, it was a tree desirable to make one intelligent through learning and reasoning using the knowledge of good and evil. This is still going on to this very day. The tree was for "knowledge" and "...*good for food, ...pleasant to the eyes and...desirable to make one wise (lehaskil)...*"

According to the threefold patterns of God, this Tree had mixed knowledge and intelligence. However, this tree did not offer one other thing they needed: Understanding! Let us see through Solomon in the following verse how understanding must be paired with wisdom. "And Your servant is in the midst of Your people whom You have chosen, a great people, too numerous to be numbered or counted. Therefore, give to Your servant *an understanding heart* to judge Your people, that *I may discern (Bin) between good and evil. For who is able to judge this great people of Yours?"* (1 Kings 3:8–9)

Though in the English it says Solomon asked for *"…an understanding heart…,"* the Hebrew text shows he asked for a *"…hearing heart…."* The English word *"understanding"* in the above passage was translated loosely from the Hebrew word *"Shama" (שָׁמַע)*, which means to hear. The Hebrew word translated as *"discern"* in the above verse is *"Bin"* (בִּין), which means to *"separate, distinguish, or perceive."* This Hebrew word also means *"between"* and is the root for the Hebrew word *"Binah,"* which is usually translated in English as Understanding. As you can see, the root of Understanding is the ability to separate. As such, Adam and Eve also needed not only to get Wisdom but also Understanding

The function of discernment is to separate things to bring order by making the right judgment. From *1 Kings 3* to *Hebrew 5*, you can see that this is a key. "For everyone who partakes only of milk is unskilled in the word of righteousness, for he is a babe. But solid food belongs to those who are of full age, that is, those who by reason of use have their senses exercised to *discern both good and evil."* (Hebrews 5:13–14)

To assist man after Adam, God appointed Judges to assist the nation of Israel with this knowledge. Judging was relegated to the *"Rulers"* of the commonwealth of Israel and this tradition can still be traced to synagogue tradition. These Rulers could be referred to as the *"Beit Din,"* which means *"House of Judgement."* The *Beit Din* were consulted to make judgments on various matters. The *Beit Din* was set up during the time of Moses: "Moreover, you shall select from all the people able men, such as fear God, men of truth, hating covetousness; and place such over them to be rulers of thousands, rulers of hundreds, rulers of fifties, and rulers of tens. And *let them judge the people at all times.* Then it will be that every great matter they shall bring to you, but every small matter *they themselves shall judge."* (Exodus 18:21–22) "And after the reading of the Law and the Prophets, *the rulers of the synagogue* sent to them, saying, "Men and brethren, if you have any word of exhortation for the people, say on." (Acts 13:15) The *Beit Din* could also be organized into a large council of Judges to what is now known as *the Sanhedrin.*

A person cannot make the right judgment until he/she has learned how to effectively discern or separate between good and evil. Also, a biased person is void of discernment and can never be a true judge. This is not about making judgments from the laws of a country. This is about making the right judgment by discerning good from evil. That is why we are encouraged not to judge because when we do, it must be a righteous judgment, not a biased or sentimental one. A right judgment is made by a careful and proper discernment between good or evil actions/intentions and making an unbiassed and appropriate ruling or judgment resulting in either a justification or condemnation. The Word of God even does this:

"For the word of God is living and powerful, and sharper than any two-edged sword, piercing even to *the division* of soul and spirit, and of joints and marrow, *and is a discerner* of the thoughts and intents of the heart." (Hebrews 4:12)

And even then, man would have to discern between good knowledge and the *"knowledge of God,"* as that specific knowledge would eventually lead him to somehow relate to God. Therefore, man can have knowledge, but he must discern between good and evil. If man is incapable of discerning the two and makes the mistake of seeing both as one, then Adam's fall is perpetuated. Man can also choose to be ignorant of knowledge but the ignorance of the knowledge of God or rejection of the knowledge of God leads to man's destruction. "My people are destroyed for lack of knowledge. Because you have rejected knowledge, I also will reject you from being priest for Me." (Hosea 4:6)

The true knowledge of God is the only knowledge that leads man towards God. Instead of going straight to the tree of life, now man was blocked from the *"Way"* to the tree. Otherwise, if Adam had been allowed to also eat from the tree of life, after his fall, the result would have looked like this:

1. His image
2. His likeness
3. *The Knowledge of Good and Evil*
4. His Life.

As you can see above, there was no way God was going to allow this to happen. There is only room for three cords in God's pattern for Adam. So, the only way man would be allowed past the cherubim was to give up the knowledge of good and evil (man's righteousness) and receive the righteousness which comes from God as a gift. This righteousness opens the *"Way"* to the *Tree of Life*.

The Separation of Light and Darkness

I want you to recall in the earlier paragraphs I mentioned that God is *pure Light*, without any shadow or darkness! The tree of the knowledge of good and evil was an anomaly: the fruit Adam and Eve ate had a *"mixture"* of *Light* (*good*) and *Darkness* (*evil*). Only God could *"separate"* the good from the evil. As such, Adam and Eve were not given the mandate or the authority to be able to separate the good from the evil mixture. During creation, God used the threefold cord of:

- *Wisdom (chochmah)*
- *Understanding (tevunah)*
- *Knowledge (daat)*.

"The Lord *by wisdom founded the earth*; By understanding (tevunah) He established the heavens; By *His knowledge*, the depths were broken up, And clouds drop down the dew." (Proverbs 3:19–20) Interestingly, this threefold cord was given to *Bezazel*, the artisan for the making of the articles of the Tabernacle of Moses: "See, I have called by name Bezalel the son of Uri, the son of Hur, of the tribe of Judah. And I have filled him with the Spirit of God, *in wisdom, in understanding, in knowledge*, and in all manner of workmanship, to design artistic works, to work in gold, in silver, in bronze, in cutting jewels for setting, in carving wood, and to work in all manner of workmanship." (Exodus 31:2–5)

Even Paul mentions this threefold pattern in the following: "…the Father of Glory, may give you the Spirit of Wisdom and Revelation in the Knowledge of Him," (Ephesians 1:17) Revelation and Understanding are the same. As you recall, Solomon asked for Wisdom and God granted it and added *great Understanding* for the purpose of discernment. "And God gave Solomon wisdom and exceedingly *great understanding* (tevunah), and largeness of heart like the sand on the seashore." (1 Kings 4:29)

The Trees in the Garden

So, during creation, God separated the light from the darkness: "And God saw the light, that it was good; and God divided (badal) the light from the darkness." (Genesis 1:4) There is an additional Hebrew word in the above verse that is not usually included and translated in the English versions. In addition to *"badal"* (בָּדַל), which means *"separate,"* the Hebrew word, *"Bayin"* (בֵּין), is included in the above verse, which means a *"space between."* Therefore, in Hebrew, it notes God separated the Light and darkness by putting *a space* between them! And this theme goes all the way into the New Testament when Paul implies that there is no communion with light or darkness:

"Do not be unequally yoked together with unbelievers. For what fellowship has righteousness with lawlessness? And what communion has light with darkness?" (2 Corinthians 6:14) Light and darkness are not meant to mix or have fellowship or communion. Light will shine where there is darkness, but the darkness cannot overtake the light. "In Him was life, and the life was the light of men. And the light shines in the darkness, and the darkness did not comprehend it." (John 1:4–6)

Light must remain pure for there to be an existence of Light! The fruit from the tree of the knowledge of good and evil had *"no space"* between *the light* from good and *the darkness* from evil. The tree did not have *"some"* fruits being good and *"some"* fruits being evil. Each of its fruit was a composite mixture of good and evil: light and darkness. The good and evil in this fruit were *one*! This mixture of (*good*) light and (*evil*) darkness, produced a type of *pseudo-light* called *"darkness,"* which leads to death because *it has no life in it* i.e., it does not have the *Light of Life.*

Consider this Scripture in which James was talking about an evil tongue: "*Does a spring send forth fresh water and bitter from the same opening? Can a fig tree, my brethren, bear olives, or a grapevine bear figs? Thus, no spring yields both salt water and fresh.*" (James 3:11–12) So, if no spring yields both salt water and fresh water, imagine how a fruit can yield both good and evil, both light and darkness!

Aspects: What You See Can Lead to What You Get

During the week of creation, the scriptures say God saw the following: "And *God saw* the light, that *it was good*; and God divided the light from the darkness." (Genesis 1:4) "And God called the dry land Earth, and the gathering together of the waters He called Seas. And *God saw* that *it was good."* (Genesis 1:10)

"Then God said, "Let the earth bring forth grass, the herb that yields seed, and the fruit tree that yields fruit according to its kind, whose seed is in itself, on the earth;" and it was so. And the earth brought forth grass, the herb that yields seed according to its kind, and the tree that yields fruit, whose seed is in itself according to its kind. And *God saw that it was good."* (Genesis 1:11–12)

"God set them in the firmament of the heavens to give light on the earth, and to rule over the day and over the night, and to divide the light from the darkness. And *God saw that it was good."* (Genesis 1:17–18)

"And God made the beast of the earth according to its kind, cattle according to its kind, and everything that creeps on the earth according to its kind. And God saw that it was good." (Genesis 1:25)

If you notice, God never said anything after creating man. However, when man was included with everything else, God saw that it was "…very good." "Then *God saw everything* that He had made, and *indeed it was very good."* (Genesis 1:31)

From the verses above, it is clear the Creator alone knows what is *"good."* God was purposeful in making sure that everything He released (light) or created was good. God was able to *"discern"* or *"judge"* what was *"good."* He did this by *dividing* or *separating* things and through His wisdom choosing the good resulting from the separations to create "order" from the chaos that was present before He began the creation. Hence the verses above keep saying *"…He saw that it was good…"* To look at the process of creation, you must observe the way God would separate things to bring about order.

Here is a refresher: He separated the light from the darkness, calling the light- Day and the darkness- Night (*Genesis 1:4*). He separated the waters by making a firmament (Heaven) between the waters above and the waters beneath the firmament (*Genesis 1:7*). By making a firmament, Heaven, He made a *separation* between Heaven and Earth. (*Genesis 1:1*). God gathered the waters into *Seas* and made dry land appear (*Genesis 1:9 & 10*). God made the plants into *three* distinct categories: grasses, herbs, and fruit trees, each with seed according to its kind (*Genesis 1:11–12*).

He created lights in the firmament of the Heavens to *divide* the day from night, for signs and seasons, between the days and years. He also made two great lights: one to rule the day and the lesser to rule the night.

He made stars to rule over both the day and night and to divide light from darkness (*Genesis 1:14–18*). Then God made a distinction between two creatures from the waters: sea creatures and all that moved within the seas and birds (Genesis 1:20–21) He created living creatures on earth according to *three* distinct categories: *cattle, creeping things, and beasts,* each according to its kind (*Genesis 1:24*). Then finally Adam, whom He created in his image but inside him, God had created a woman, whom He would *separate* from within Adam (*Genesis 1:27 & Genesis 2:23*).

As you can see, the process of creation was a careful and deliberate process to bring order through dividing and separation or *"discerning."* God would use wisdom to divide and discern from the division, what was good. This process of division to bring order is the process of *"Judgement,"* which is displayed through the Bible. As you can see below King Solomon who was gifted with wisdom said the following: "Therefore give to Your servant an understanding (shama: שָׁמַע) heart to judge (shaphat: שָׁפַט) Your people, that I may *discern* (bin: בִּין) *between good and evil*. For who is able to judge this great people of Yours?" (1 Kings 3:9)

The Hebrew word *"shama"* above means to *"hear and obey."* For one to judge, he/she must have a *"listening heart"* so that they can *"discern"* between good and evil. "But solid food belongs to those who are of full age, that is, those who by reason of use have their senses exercised to *discern both good and evil*." (Hebrews 5:14)

Righteous judgment involves a process of *separation,* between good and evil, which is given through wisdom by a listening heart: a heart listening to God. If a person is unable to listen to God, they will be unable to discern or make the separation between good and evil. Such a person cannot be able to judge according to Heaven. In courtrooms, Judges make decisions by interpreting the *"laws"* governing their authority. It is another thing altogether if they can separate between actual good and evil.

So, when the Bible states the following below about the *Word of God*, it is giving you notice that the function of the Word of God is to *separate* so chaos is removed, and order can come into your life for good.

"For the word of God is living and powerful, and sharper than any two-edged sword, *piercing even to the division* of soul and spirit, and of joints and marrow, and is a *discerner* of the thoughts and intents of the heart. And there is no creature hidden from His sight, but all things are naked and open to the eyes of Him to whom we must give account." (Hebrews 4:12–13)

The Word of God discerns both good and evil, in the thoughts and intents of the heart. If you allow it to separate the good from the evil, then you are ready for order in your life, and you will declare that the will of God in your life is *"...good, acceptable, and perfect..."* (Romans 12:2).

With the above examples, it was important from the very beginning for man to have God's judgment on everything. Adam did not even discern that being alone was not in his best interest. God is the one who *saw* that Adam needed a partner. "And the Lord God said, "It is *not good* that man should be alone; I will make him a helper comparable to him." Out of the ground the Lord God formed every beast of the field and every bird of the air and brought them to Adam to see what he would call them. And whatever Adam called each living creature, that was its name. So, Adam gave names to all cattle, to the birds of the air, and to every beast of the field. But for Adam there was not found a helper comparable to him." (Genesis 2:18-22)

If you notice above, God states first that He would make Adam comparable helper, then He brings every *"beast of the field"* and *"bird of the air"* to Adam to *'see'* what he would call them. After Adam names both groups, the Biblical portion still ends with the phrase, *"...But for Adam there was not found a helper comparable to him...."* Wasn't Adam supposed to just name the animals and birds? That phrase shows Adam may have been looking as it says, *"But for Adam there was not found..."* Not Found? who was looking? Certainly not God, as He had already decided to *"...make Adam a comparable helper..."* before naming the animals.

It seems Adam had picked up God's perspective on the matter though he had not been explicitly told. God was seeing if Adam may call any of the animals or birds his comparable helper. However, Adam passed by naming the animals and birds and not naming any as comparable to him. This was a test of whether Adam had God's perspective on what is "good" for Adam! Adam was made in the image of God. He had to find a helper that was made in the same image or likeness.

Also, God knew Adam's *"type"* as we may say. God created Adam. He knew what kind of woman Adam would like because He knew *what was good* for Adam. That is why when Adam saw Eve for the first time, he *called* her differently from the names he had given the animals and birds. She was perfect for him. God knows what is good for us. Adam said, *"...she shall be called Woman because she was taken out of man..."* (Genesis 2:23). So how is this relevant to where we are going? Well, it was having God's perspective and holding onto it that may have saved Adam and Eve from eating from the Tree of the knowledge of good and evil. This was God's perspective on the matter of that tree: "And the Lord God commanded the man, saying, "Of every tree of the garden you may freely eat; but of the tree of the knowledge of good and evil *you shall not eat*, for in the day that you eat of it *you shall surely die*." (Genesis 2:16-17)

Why was it important for Adam to keep God's perspective? Because Adam had not been given the ability to *discern* between Good and Evil. However, the snake was successful in changing Eve's perspective away from God's perspective. It was a change from depending upon God's perspective to depending upon her own, independent perspective. "So, when *the woman saw* that *the tree was good for food*, that *it was pleasant to the eyes*, and a *tree desirable to make one wise*, she took of its fruit and ate. She also gave to her husband with her, and he ate." (Genesis 3:6)

Instead of the narrative saying, "...*God saw...*," now it was stating, "...*the woman saw....*" This tree of which God said that if they ate from it, "...*you shall surely die...*" was now "...*pleasant to the eyes....*" Regardless of what God had said, in her eyes, the tree was now "...*good for food...*" and "...*desirable to make one wise....*" "Woe to those who call evil good, and good evil; who put darkness for light, and light for darkness; who put bitter for sweet, and sweet for bitter! Woe to those *who are wise in their own eyes, And prudent in their own sight!*" (Isaiah 5:20-21)

If only Isaiah had been there to warn them of the danger of straying from God's perspective.

Adam's Eyes being opened

The serpent knowing the fruit of this tree wanted Adam and Eve's eyes to be opened to this mixture because he knew the result. The *lie* to Adam and Eve was that if their eyes would be opened by the fruit of this tree, they would be like God. "Then the serpent said to the woman, "You will not surely die. For God knows that in the day you eat of it *your eyes will be opened*, and you will be like God, *knowing good and evil*." (Genesis 3:4-5)

Opened to what? To see both light (good) and darkness (evil) *as one*. Picture your eyes not being focused on one thing but on two things at the same time. This sinister plot by the snake to open their eyes is made very clear "Then the eyes of both of them were opened, and they knew that they were naked." (Genesis 3:6-7)

The English word *"both"* in the above verse is translated from the Hebrew word *"shettayim"* (שְׁנַיִם), which is the *"cardinal number two."* The Hebrew word for *"both"* is *"yachad"* (יַחַד), which was *not* used in the above verse. In English, it could make sense, but in Hebrew, the difference in the words used to me sometimes changes the meaning of what is being described. So, the verse should look more like, *"…And were opened the eyes as two (double), and they knew…."* The eyes opened to *two agendas* (good and evil).

Opening the eye to two agendas has great implications. Look at what Yeshua when He says below: "The lamp of the body is the eye. If therefore your eye is good, your whole body will be full of light. But if your eye is bad, your whole body will be full of darkness. *If therefore the light that is in you is darkness, how great is that darkness!"* (Matthew 6:22–23)

This passage can be a bit confusing, but the Greek text makes it clear considering we are talking about the tree of the knowledge of good and evil. In *Matthew 6:22*, the Greek word translated in English as *"good"* is *"haplous,"* which means *"single"* or *"a single fold"*: without a (secret) *"double agenda"*, while in verse *twenty-three*, the Greek word translated in English as *"bad"* is *"ponéros"* also translated as *"evil"* in other New Testament Bible verses, which means *"hardships, labors and annoyances."* Notice, though most English translations will say "bad," the Greek always shows the word *"evil." The biblical opposite of good is evil!* This is confirmed by the King James Version (KJV) of the same verse. "The light of the body is the eye: if therefore *thine eye be single*, thy whole body shall be full of light. But if thine eye be evil, thy whole body shall be full of darkness. If therefore the light that is in thee be darkness, how great is that darkness!" (Matthew 6:22–23 (KJV))

Yeshua explains further about not having a mixture of light and darkness: "Therefore *take heed that the light which is in you is not darkness*. If then your whole body is full of light, *having no part dark*, the whole body will be full of light, as when the bright shining of a lamp gives you light." (Luke 11:35–36)

The tree of the knowledge of good and evil has a *"double agenda,"* that is *good and evil!* Therefore, the *Light* created from that tree is a mixture of good and evil, which produces darkness, which leads to death as there is no life in the darkness. The serpent's aim of opening their eyes was to see the effect on the *"light in their bodies."* So, when their eyes were opened to both light and darkness, their bodies would be filled with a pseudo-light called darkness. That is why Yeshua says in Matthew 6:23, *"...If therefore the light that is in you is darkness, how great is that darkness..."*

However, the tree of life is *singular* in focus: its fruit is all about *one* thing, *life*! Even Yeshua said in *John 10:10*, *"...I have come that you may have life, and life more abundantly...."* He did not say *"...life and..."* something else. He said, *"...Life and Life...,"* which equals *life*. The emphasis on life was the abundance of it. Therefore, had Adam and Eve eaten from the tree of life, their bodies would have been full of Light, as the Bible notes *Life has its source in Light* as well: "Behold, God works all these things, Twice, in fact, three times with a man, To bring back his soul from the Pit, That he may be enlightened with the *light of life*." (Job 33:29–31)

So, know that anytime there is a *double agenda* or *multiple folds* involving *contradicting* views without the aim of producing absolute good, the result will always be darkness, which leads to death. The Tree of the knowledge of good and evil has a double agenda: its *"double-minded."* Being double-minded is not a compliment in Scripture. Have a look at the following verses: "I hate the double-minded, But I love Your law." (Psalm 119:113 ס *SAMEK*) The Hebrew word for the English word, *"double-minded"* in the above verse is *"Seeph"* (סֵעֲפִים), which is also translated as *"halfhearted"* or *"divided."* "For let not that man suppose that he will receive anything from the Lord; he is a *double-minded man, unstable in all his ways*." (James 1:7-8)

Interestingly, the above verse states that a double-minded man is *"... unstable in all his ways."* You can imagine how Adam and Eve had become in one instant: *unstable in all their ways* as now they carried both a *good mind* and an *evil mind*! "Therefore, submit to God. Resist the devil and he will flee from you. Draw near to God and He will draw near to you. Cleanse your hands, you sinners and purify your hearts, *you double-minded*." (James 4:7-8)

Adam and Eve having both eaten the fruit of this tree were now full of darkness and were no longer reflecting God's image or likeness.

Becoming like God knowing Good and Evil?

As a result of them eating from the tree of the knowledge of good and evil, it is noted that God says the following, "Behold, *the man has become like one of Us, to know good and evil*. And now, lest he put out his hand and take also of the tree of life, and eat, and live forever" therefore the Lord God sent him out of the garden of Eden to till the ground from which he was taken.

The Supernatural Ways of God

So, He drove out the man; and He placed cherubim at the east of the garden of Eden, and a flaming sword which turned every way, to *guard the Way to the tree of life...*" (Genesis 3:21–24)

Please know, the phrase, "...*man has become like one of us to know good and evil...*" was not translated from the Hebrew text and it gives the wrong impression about what God said. The verse shows the following in the Hebrew text: *The phrase* "...*has become...*" was translated from one Hebrew word, *"Hayah,"* which means *to "exist," "to be," "to become"* but also *"to fallout"*

The part, "...*like one...*" was translated from one Hebrew word, *"Echad"* (אֶחָד), which means, *"being One"*! It is the same Hebrew word used in the following popular verse: *Deuteronomy 6:4: "Hear, O Israel: The Lord our God, the Lord is One* (אֶחָד:)*!*

The part "...*of us...*" was translated from one Hebrew word, *"Min,"* which means *"From"*

And "...*to know...*" was translated from one Hebrew word, *"Yada,"* which means *"to know"* or become aware

As you can see from the Hebrew text, I am certain God meant something like this, "...*man has fallen out of One(-ness) with Us, knowing good and evil....*" Man fell from being one with God (sharing his Glory) when he received the knowledge of good and evil. Man lost the Glory of God, which had previously allowed man to be *One* with God. To further confirm that the phrase "...*become like one of us...*" from the English translation is questionable, the *Targums* of the Torah by *Onkelos* notes the verse as follows:

"And the Lord God Said, Behold, man is become singular (or alone, yechid) in the world by himself, knowing good and evil..."[4]

Adam became the *single being* or *alone* in all of creation to know good and evil. Therefore, Adam was no longer connected to God. He *fell out* of union with God, i.e., he fell out of the Glory of God. When he fell, everything out of him fell. *When he fell, we all fell!* "for *all* have sinned and *fall short of the glory of God*," (Romans 3:23)

The Glory of God is what unifies us with God as noted by Yeshua "And *the glory* which You gave Me *I have given them,* that *they may be One just as We are One*: I in them, and You in Me; that they may be made perfect in One," (John 17:22–23) I am sure Yeshua said the Hebrew word *"Echad"* when HE said "One" in the above verses. Adam and Eve were covered before eating the forbidden fruit. "Then the eyes of both of them were opened,

---

4. Etheridge, *The Targums*, 42.

and they knew that they were naked; and they sewed fig leaves together and made themselves covering." (Genesis 3:7)

The above verse does not show *"gain"* as ones who *became like God*. The verse shows great loss: their eyes saw *"shame"* instead of innocence, which caused them to make *"...themselves coverings..."*! Why? They were previously naked as noted below (before they ate from the forbidden tree) but were not ashamed. "And they were both naked, the man and his wife, and *were not ashamed."* (Genesis 2:25)

They were not ashamed because they were *covered in God's Glory*. They were naked *and* covered in God's Glory! However, when they ate the fruit, they exchanged his Glory for shame. So, they were naked and covered in shame! "Hear me when I call, O God of my righteousness! You have relieved me in my distress Have mercy on me and hear my prayer. How long, O you sons of men, *Will you turn my glory to shame*? How long will you love worthlessness And seek falsehood? Selah" (Psalm 4:1–2)

The Biblical opposite of Glory is *Shame*: "You are filled with *shame instead of glory.* You also—drink! And be exposed as uncircumcised! The cup of the Lord's right hand will be turned against you, And utter shame will be on your glory." (Habakkuk 2:16) "My people are destroyed for lack of knowledge. Because you have rejected knowledge, I also will reject you from being priest for Me; Because you have forgotten the law of your God, I also will forget your children. "The more they increased, The more they sinned against Me; *I will change their glory into shame."* (Hosea 4:6–7)

There is a difference between *"being naked and covered in Glory"* and *"being naked and covered in shame."* They did not become like God while being covered in shame! That is why I believe the Hebrew word, *"hayah"* as noted previously could have meant *"to fall out."* They *"...fell short of the Glory..."* because now they were filled with darkness and covered in shame. There was a separation between God and man immediately upon Adam receiving the knowledge of good and evil: Adam and Eve *fell out of the Glory of God*. Adam could not be *One* (*"Echad"*) with God when he took on darkness in himself because, in God, there is no darkness.

Parable of the Fig Tree

Adam and Eve had both been *"blind"* having *no knowledge* of good or evil: they were innocent! Their innocence was given to them by God when they were both created. However, now that they had an intimate knowledge of good and evil and self-will to choose between the two choices, they lost all innocence! Feeling shame, they covered themselves with sewed *"fig leaves"* and hid from God. You certainly do not hide from the *One Whom* you have become like. On the contrary, they were hiding because now they realized they were *no longer* like Him.

"Then the *eyes of both of them were opened*, and they knew that they were naked; and they sewed *fig leaves* together and made themselves coverings. And they heard the sound of the Lord God walking in the garden in the cool of the day, and Adam and his wife hid themselves from *the presence of the Lord God* among the trees of the garden. Then the Lord God called to Adam and said to him, "Where are you?" So, he said, "I heard Your voice in the garden, and I was afraid because I was naked; and I hid myself." (Genesis 3:7–10)

They lost the Glory of God, and both sensed the *"innocence"* in them evaporate. Their eyes were aware of good and evil. As the light within them was now darkness, they had to hide what was within by covering what was on the outside. Interestingly, they used *fig leaves* to cover up: I will talk about the fig tree in a little bit. The above scriptures state they his themselves from the *"…Presence of the LORD God…."* Please note, the English word, "Presence" in the above verse is translated from the Hebrew word *"panim or paneh,"* which means *"face"* or *"faces"*! They both hid from the *"Face of LORD God"*: due to shame. (Sidenote: Picture in Hebrew terms what you are asking for when you request the *Presence* of the LORD God. You are asking for his face!)

In the Book of Judges, a man by the name of Jotham gives an interesting parable about the trees going to four different trees to anoint a King over them. Please notice the difference between the fig tree's response compared to the other three trees:

"Now when they told Jotham, he went and stood on top of Mount Gerizim, and lifted his voice and cried out. And he said to them: "Listen to me, you men of Shechem, That God may listen to you! "The trees once went forth to anoint a king over them.

And they said to the *olive tree*, 'Reign over us!' But the olive tree said to them, 'Should I cease giving my oil, *With which they honor God and men*, And go to sway over trees?' "Then the trees said to the *fig tree*,

'You come and reign over us!' But the fig tree said to them, '*Should I cease my sweetness and my good fruit*, And go to sway over trees?' "Then the trees said to the *vine*, 'You come and reign over us!'

But the vine said to them, 'Should I cease my new wine, *Which cheers both God and men*, And go to sway over trees?' "Then all the trees said to the *bramble*, 'You come and reign over us!' And the bramble said to the trees, 'If in truth you anoint me as king over you, *Then come and take shelter in my shade*; But if not, let fire come out of the bramble And devour the cedars of Lebanon!' (Judges 9:7–15)

The olive tree and the vine are noted in the above verses for the product of their fruits specifically used to foster a *relationship* between God and man by assisting in bringing *"honor"* and *"cheers"* for *"…both God and men…."* That is why God called Israel a *Green Olive Tree* and a *Noble Vine*: "The Lord called your name, Green Olive Tree, lovely and of Good Fruit…." (Jeremiah 11:16) "Yet I had planted you a noble vine, a seed of highest quality…" (Jeremiah 2:21) However, the fig tree does not assist in fostering a relationship between God and men. It serves itself due to *"…my sweetness and my good fruit…."* This tree represents the *individual person* as a *"fig,"* which has "sweetness" and is "good fruit."

This fig is a person of wisdom through learning, has pleasant words of counsel and has good in him/her: "The wise in heart will be called prudent, And sweetness of the lips increases learning" (Proverbs 16:21) The sweetness of the lips is pleasant words and hearty counsel: "Pleasant words are like a honeycomb, Sweetness to the soul and health to the bones." (Proverbs 16:24) "And the sweetness of a man's friend gives delight by hearty counsel." (Proverbs 27:9) Fruit is what comes out of a person. The fig can either be good or bad. "Either make the tree good and its fruit good, or else make the tree bad and its fruit bad; *for a tree is known by its fruit.*" (Matthew 12:33)

"Beware of false prophets, who come to you in sheep's clothing, but inwardly they are ravenous wolves. You will know them by their fruits. Do men gather grapes from thornbushes or figs from thistles? Even so, every good tree bears good fruit, but a bad tree bears bad fruit. A good tree cannot bear bad fruit, nor can a bad tree bear good fruit. Every tree that does not bear good fruit is cut down and thrown into the fire. Therefore, by their fruits you will know them." (Matthew 7:15–20)

So, a "fig" is a person who attempts to be righteous through learning. So, in the case of the trees, the fig tree is trying to produce *sweetness* and *good fruit* for itself. So that when a person eats its fruit (experiences), they can say it is sweet and it was good. This is the tree from which Adam and Eve sewed leaves for a covering (Genesis 3:7). What the leaves were covering was their lack of sweetness and good fruit.

A *fruit tree* without fruits is naked! So, it will use leaves to cover its nakedness. When the fruits are ready, it will display openly its fruits to be looked at and to be eaten. Their sweetness and good fruit (now mixed with evil) disappeared and so they were naked. And like a fruit tree without fruit, they covered themselves with the fig leaves. And this *false covering* has been on man ever since. Yeshua deals with this covering by confronting the fig tree for not producing fruit.

"Now the next day, when they had come out from Bethany, He was hungry. And seeing from afar a fig tree having leaves, He went to see if perhaps He would find something on it. When He came to it, He found nothing but leaves, for it was not the season for figs. In response Jesus said to it, "Let no one eat fruit from you ever again." And His disciples heard it…. Now in the morning, as they passed by, they saw the fig tree dried up from the roots. And Peter, remembering, said to Him, "Rabbi, look! The fig tree which You cursed has withered away." So, Jesus answered and said to them, "Have faith in God. For assuredly, I say to you, whoever says to this mountain, 'Be removed and be cast into the sea,' and does not doubt in his heart, but believes that those things he says will be done, he will have whatever he says." (Mark 11:12–14; 20–23)

Yeshua was not just cursing an ordinary tree because it did not give Him fruit to eat. He went way beyond that. He was dealing with the effects of the *'false covering of self-righteousness'* provided by the *"leaves"* of this tree, which man was still covering himself since Adam. The issue was no fruit. The leaves make other men believe there is fruit underneath. God requires sweet and good *"fruit in all seasons*. The *Tree of Life* produces fruit in all seasons and even its leaves are not just for covering but for healing: "In the middle of its street, and on either side of the river, was the tree of life, which bore twelve fruits, each tree yielding its fruit every month. The leaves of the tree were for the healing of the nations." (Revelation 22:2)

While you are trying to better yourself through study, know that God is requiring fruit in your life. "He also spoke this parable: "A certain man had a fig tree planted in his vineyard, and he came seeking fruit on it and found none. Then he said to the keeper of his vineyard, 'Look, for three years I have come seeking fruit on this fig tree and find none. Cut it down; why does it use up the ground?' But he answered and said to him, 'Sir, let it alone this year also, until I dig around it and fertilize it." (Luke 13:6–8)

Many have leaves and God keeps coming searching for sweet, good fruit and all He finds are leaves. The verse says the fig tree was planted in his vineyard. You can be in the house of God studying to improve yourself, which is great! However, He needs to find pleasant fruit on your tree.

When Yeshua says, *"Have faith in God,"* He means look towards God to help you produce fruit or be fruitful and your leaves should be leaves healing the nations. "I am the vine; you are the branches. He who abides in Me, and I in him, bears much fruit; for without Me you can do nothing." (John 15:5) Also note, when He says, *"...whoever says to this mountain, 'Be removed...',"* He was in context, referring to the fig tree as a mountain that should be removed! Why does He refer to it as a mountain?

This is a metaphor. Let me explain by using the following verse: "I will lift up my eyes to the hills From whence comes my help?" (Psalm 121:1) In the New Living Translation (NLT), the word *"mountains"* is used instead of *"hills"* in this verse by the New King James Version. Mountains can be used because it is translated from the Hebrew phrase, *"he-harim"* (הֶהָרִים), which means *"the mountains."* The Hebrew word for mountain is *"har"* (הַר) and mountains in the plural is *"harim"* (הָרִים).

To explain what Yeshua meant by *this mountain*, the Rabbis note in *Bereshit Rabbah 68:2*, which states, *"...Rabbi Samuel Bar Nachman opened [his homiletic exposition with the following verses]: "A song for ascents. I lift my eyes to the mountains (harim)." (Ps 121:1) [Read the verse] I lift my eyes to my parents (horim), meaning my forebears and my teachers."*[5]

In the above, Rabbi Nachman is saying instead of reading the verse as *"harim"* (for mountains), you should read it as *"horim,"* which means *"parents"* or *"teachers."* Why? Because they say this verse was Jacob lifting his eyes towards his *Fathers* (Abraham and Isaac) who are *"spiritual mountains"* or *"spiritual fathers"* from whom he learned the things of God. So, using this metaphor, if Yeshua says, *"...whoever says to this mountain, 'Be removed and be cast into the sea ...,"* He was talking about the *"false covering of the fig leaves"* being *your teacher*, who needs to be removed and cast out into the sea!

He was not talking about a physical mountain being cast into the sea! Even with all the miracles He did, He never moved an entire mountain into the sea. There was no reason to do that. In the *Jastrow Dictionary* (A dictionary of the Talmud and Targumim by Marcus Jastrow), under "תְּאֵנָה" or *"fig-tree,"* it states, "...תחת ת' אחת ... היו ...*were wont to rise early and sit down under a certain fig-tree to study....*" So, sitting under a fig tree was

---

5. Talmudic Israel/Babylon, *Bereishit Rabbah* 68:2.

known as *a place to study*. That explains why Yeshua said the following about Nathanael:

"Jesus saw Nathanael coming toward Him, and said of him, "Behold, an Israelite indeed, in whom is no deceit!" Nathanael said to Him, "How do You know me?" Jesus answered and said to him, "Before Philip called you, when you were under the fig tree, I saw you." (John 1:47–48)

Nathaniel was a man of study. As we noted earlier, he was also a person who had sweetness and good fruit. That is why Yeshua said, *"...in whom is no deceit..."* If he was a man of study, it means he had a teacher or Spiritual father (*Mountain*) from whom he was learning.

So, when Yeshua was searching for figs, He could not find any because the tree was not producing righteousness or *righteous people* (figs)! The teachings of the day were not producing people with good fruit. So, he *cursed* the system from the roots! That mountain has already been cast into the sea. So, if you are operating from this system, you are operating from a curse!

Just a side note: it is also interesting that the Jastrow Dictionary under *"fig -tree"* also states, "...בעל התי' יודע וכ'. the *owner of the fig-tree knows when it is time to pluck it (God knows when it is time to call the righteous away) ....*"

If plucking the fig tree represents when *God is going to pluck the righteous*, it makes sense when He later says: "Then they will see the Son of Man coming in the clouds with great power and glory. And then He will send His angels, and gather together His elect from the four winds, from the farthest part of earth to the farthest part of heaven. "Now learn this parable from the fig tree: When its branch has already become tender, and puts forth leaves, you know that summer is near. So, you also when you see these things happening, know that it is near—at the doors!" (Mark 13:26–29)

Your teachers can be *mountains* in your life. When you remove the *false covering of self-righteousness* as your teacher, He then says, *"...have faith in God..."* Why? God will be your teacher! "Take My yoke upon you and learn from Me, for I am gentle and lowly in heart, and you will find rest for your souls." (Matthew 11:29)

By choosing the one tree, Adam and Eve lost the entire garden and access to the one tree they needed to eat from i.e., the tree of life was now forbidden. Anytime we chose a *"way"* independent of God, even though it seems right, it will end in the *"way of death."* "There is a way that seems right to a man, But its end is the way of death." (Proverbs 14:12)

As Adam and Eve were now traversing the *way of death*, it seemed right for the Lord to create a *"way"* to the *Tree of Life*. The way of the Lord was clear; it was the *Way of Righteousness* leading to the tree of life. "In the *Way of Righteousness is Life*, And in its pathway *there is no death*." (Proverbs 12:28)

The *Way of Righteousness* was already available to them. This "path" or *"Way"* was created by God, not man! The last Adam created this path. This path had only one end: *The Tree of Life*. God created the tree of life. As such, eating from the tree of life was free: it was *a gift*, from the beginning!

Therefore, if the fruit of the tree of life given by God could only be reached by one path that He had created, it means there was *no other way* to get to the tree of life. If you also notice, there was no *"path"* to the tree of the knowledge of good and evil, which means Adam had to find his own way to get to the tree. The serpent through seduction and deception provided a "way" for them: the way of death! This way seemed *"...right to a man..."* and they ate from the tree of the knowledge of good and evil.

The Covering of Fig leaves

As you know, Adam and Eve were both thrown out of the garden and the way was being guarded from them. From the onset of eating from that tree, man has tried to show themselves as being *'good'* and always avoids being seen as *'evil.'* To put it in modern terms, it is so ingrained in us to greet with the words *"...Good morning!"* We want the morning to be good! We ask, *"...How are you?"* What is our response? *"...I'm good..."* You rarely hear anyone respond by saying, *"...I'm evil...."* Most people will say, *"...I am a good person...I am a good husband! ...I am a good wife...I am a good worker...I am a good citizen...I am good...I am good...I am good."*

Rarely do you hear the use of the word 'evil' to describe oneself. It is so rarely used that only *"Dr. Evil"* in the Austin Powers movies dares to call himself evil. Normally you will hear the occasional use of the word *"bad."* *"...He is a bad worker...he is a bad husband...she is a bad wife..."* The word *evil* is specially reserved for infamous people like Adolf Hitler. However, this Tree does not have a neutral position: it is *not* the Tree of the knowledge of *Good, Bad and Evil*.

You have only two options: *either you are good*, or *you are evil!* Either the news you are watching is *good* news or *evil* news. Either the report you are receiving is a good report or an evil report. Either the work you are doing is excellent work or evil work. Please do not misunderstand there are levels of darkness: there is darkness and "deep" darkness. There is not a significant number of people I know in Hitler's level of darkness, however, know that if what a person is doing is *not good*, it is in the opposite category of the tree: *it is evil*!

The Light from the Tree of the Knowledge of Good and Evil

As Yeshua said, *"…If therefore the light that is in you is darkness, how great is that darkness!"* The Tree was the source of light different from the pure light of God. Man was now always trying to prove his/her innocence: the sense that their decision to be good and not be evil would entail their innocence. However, how do you show that you are good? By the things man does! The Tree of the knowledge of good and evil is the source of all *"self-innocence"* or *"self-righteousness"* i.e., a righteousness from man, not of God!

This tree is the source of *all self-dependence,* where one makes *choices* that are independent of God's guidance. It is a tree whose fruit caused man to attain righteousness or lack thereof by his *"choices"* between good or evil. This tree is the source of most religious activity around the world, where man attempts to ascend spirituality to a state of righteousness based solely on the choices made between good and evil.

Because of this tree, man has devised lists of things "to do" to become righteous! Even in simple everyday examples, people will tell you the things they "do" to prove why they are good: *"I'm a good person…because I pay my taxes…because I vote…because I feed my children…because I keep my house clean…because I meditate everyday…because I'm committed to my job…because I have been faithful to my husband…because I paid my children's college tuition…"* The things listed above are all good things to do and the list can go on and on, but it is not enough for the person to be called, *"righteous"*!

If these are not even close, what other things can one *"do"* to bring them to that level called righteousness? *Building a skyscraper? Becoming a billionaire? Shutting the world off and becoming a monk? Doing exercises and staying fit? Eating only organic food? Doing yoga every morning? Speaking positively all day? Joining the Navy seals and fighting for your country? Making sure you are dressed decently not showing any skin? Being a truthful news anchor? Volunteering at the local food pantry every week? Giving away all my clothes to goodwill?*

The Trees in the Garden

All these may seem good things but sorry for the shock: none of these things pass the test of being righteous! There is no list on the earth that I can give you that you can do to become righteous! This was the dilemma from the time Adam ate the fruit: how was man going to attain righteousness now that it was lost? There seemed to be a solution in sight for man by the time Moses showed up in time.

Chapter 6

From Filthy Rags to Glorious Garments

Moshe's Law of Righteousness

Please remember, God did teach Abraham the way of righteousness: you become Righteous when you believe God and He gives you, his righteousness. As I am assuming many will read the Bible for themselves, I will not go into too much detail about the period between Abraham and Moses. However, 430 years after Abraham, God had given the children of Israel the Law of Moses (Moshe). Two things had happened: While in Egypt's captivity, they had lost or forgotten the way of righteousness.

God needed to correctly define what was truly good and what was truly evil. He also needed to deal with the tree of the knowledge of good and evil by showing that no matter what man did or did not do, there is but one way of righteousness. As man needed things *"to do"* to become righteous, God provided the children of Israel with 613 commandments to follow to earn righteousness. As you see below, Moses advised them they had all they needed to *"do it"* and had to make *"a choice."*

"if you obey the voice of the Lord your God, to keep His commandments and His statutes which are written in this *Book of the Law*, and if you turn to the Lord your God with all your heart and with all your soul. "For this commandment which I command you today is not too mysterious for you, nor is it far off. It is not in heaven, that you should say, 'Who will ascend into heaven for us and bring it to us, that we may hear it and do it? Nor is it beyond the sea, that you should say, 'Who will go over the sea for us and bring it to us, that we may hear it and *do it*?' But the word is very near you, in your mouth and in your heart, that you *may do it*. "See, I have set before you today *life and good, death and evil,* in that I command you today to love the Lord your God, to walk in His ways, and to keep His commandments, His statutes, and His judgments, that you may live and multiply; and the Lord your God will bless you in the land which you go to possess." (Deuteronomy 30:10–16)

"I call heaven and earth as witnesses today against you, that I have set before you *life and death, blessing and cursing;* therefore *choose life,* that both you and your descendants may live; that you may love the Lord your God, that you may obey His voice, and that you may cling to Him, for He is your life and the length of your days; and that you may dwell in the land which the Lord swore to your fathers, to Abraham, Isaac, and Jacob, to give them." (Deuteronomy 30:19–20)

Here is a picture of what Moses said in verses 15 and 19, choose

LIFE	death
good	evil
blessing	cursing

In summary, they could choose Life *by doing* good and receiving blessing that they and their descendants may live and dwell in the land God swore to their fathers (Abraham, Isaac, and Jacob) to give them, otherwise, they could choose death, *by doing* evil and receiving cursing. To give credit to the children of Israel, no nation would have been able to keep all the commandments perfectly. So as the Bible details, it is obvious they failed to keep the Law of Moses.

Again, this is not a rebuke to the children of Israel; all nations given the same commandments would have failed. Why? No nation or person can attain righteousness by the things they do or the choices they make between good or evil. The Bible states the generation Moses led failed to cross into the promised land except for Joshua and Caleb. Here is a little clue as to why God chose the next generation to cross into the promised land:

"Joshua the son of Nun, who stands before you, he shall go in there. Encourage him, for he shall cause Israel to inherit it. 'Moreover, your little ones and your children, who you say will be victims, who *today have no knowledge of good and evil, they shall go in there*; to them I will give it, and they shall possess it. But as for you, turn and take your journey into the wilderness by the way of the Red Sea.'" (Deuteronomy 1:38–40)

The knowledge of good and evil is never a key to inheriting the things of God. As you can see above, *the lack* of the knowledge of good and evil *was the key* to inheriting the promised land. The generation God spoke of above knew nothing but total dependence on God, not on their strength, ability, or choice. The nation of Israel was missing the revelation of the way of the Lord by this time!

In the generations following Joseph, they lost the understanding of the way of the Lord, which should have been passed down without any changes. However, not only was the understanding of the way of the Lord misunderstood as time passed, but those that passed it down perverted it. God needed prophets to prophesy about the coming messenger, John as we learned earlier, to correct their understanding and to prepare them for the coming of the Messiah.

The Spiritual Nature of Self-Righteousness

Just as Adam covered himself in fig leaves, the Prophet Isaiah saw the pitiful condition and nature of self-righteousness and what it looks like:

"But we are all like an unclean thing, And *all our righteousnesses* are like *filthy rags*; We all fade as a leaf, And our iniquities, like the wind, Have taken us away." (Isaiah 64:6)

When he says *"all our righteousness's"* he means all. Even the English spelling of the word *"righteousness's"* in this verse implies they are more than one, *multiple* or even *numerous* in number. So, we have produced varied types of righteousness's! The world has many diverse types and forms of *righteousness's* defined by the varied traditional beliefs and religions. We will not go into those details. The Hebrew word translated as *"all"* is the word, *"kol"* (כֹּל), which means *"whole."*

The *whole lot* of our varied *righteousness's* are as filthy rags. The word *"filthy"* is translated from the Hebrew word *"iddim"* (עִדִּים). This is derived from the Hebrew word *"ed"* (עֵד), which is connected to *menstruation*. However, what is particularly interesting is that this word can also mean *"witness"* in Hebrew. So, in the plural, *'iddim'* can also mean *"witnesses"* as the verse speaks of *'righteousness's'* in the plural. The word *"rags"* is translated from the Hebrew word *"begged"* (בֶּגֶד), which comes from the Hebrew root word *"bagad"* (בָּגַד) meaning *"to deal treacherously"* and *"to cover."*

So, self-righteousness is *covering oneself with a garment of treachery*. Even more plainly, our *self-righteousness's* are *"witnesses of our garments of*

From Filthy Rags to Glorious Garments

treachery." Because of this, the verse says, *"…we all fade as a leaf…."* The phrase noted in English in the above verse as *"…we all fade…"* is the Hebrew word, *"nabel"* (נָבֵל), which means *"disgrace/foolish, which comes to nothing."* This Hebrew word also means *"wither."*

When a leaf withers, the tree or plant discard it and it is usually blown away by the wind. It becomes irrelevant. Therefore, all attempts to become righteousness through our own efforts are like covering ourselves with *filthy rags* or *garments of treachery*, which leads to disgrace, and foolishness and comes to nothing! We wither away from the source and are impressed by the wind into irrelevance! Why? There is nothing we can *"do"* on our own to become as *"innocent as God"*!

And just to let you know, the devil loves when we walk in self-righteousness because it was by his deception that Adam ate from the tree and man fell into condemnation by becoming self-righteousness. Even when we are doing things for God, if we walk in self-righteousness, satan, is there to oppose us. See below what happened to Joshua the High Priest as the Prophet Zechariah saw in the Spirit.

"Then he showed me Joshua *the high priest* standing before the Angel of the Lord, and Satan standing at his right hand *to oppose him.* And the Lord said to Satan, "The Lord rebuke you, Satan! The Lord who has chosen Jerusalem rebuke you! Is this not a brand plucked from the fire?" Now Joshua was *clothed with filthy garments* and was standing before the Angel. Then He answered and spoke to those who stood before Him, saying, *"Take away the filthy garments from him."* And to him He said, "See, *I have removed your iniquity from you, and I will clothe you with rich robes."* (Zechariah 3:1-4)

The accuser will stand at your right hand *to oppose you* when you are carrying *"filthy garments,"* which according to Isaiah chapter 60 represents *"our"* righteousness. In the above passage, the word *"filthy"* is translated from a different Hebrew word, *"hatzoim"* (הַצֹּאִים), whose root would be translated as *"soiled."* Soiled as in a sense of being stained with excrement! Joshua is the High Priest; this is serious. Recall God said to the children of Israel the following about the Priestly garments: "And you shall make holy garments for Aaron your brother, for glory and for beauty" (Exodus 28:2)

Joshua's garments were supposed to be glorious and beautiful, however, he showed up with them looking soiled! What caused them to be soiled? Iniquity! It is easy to cover ourselves with *"other"* garments when we walk outside of God's righteousness. Was Joshua an evil man? That is not my conclusion, but it does say his *"iniquity"* was taken away. In Isaiah 64:6, it does say, *"...And our iniquities, like the wind, have taken us away...."* In Joshua's case, the Hebrew word translated from *"...your iniquity..."* in the passage was *"avoneka"* (עֲוֹנֶךָ), which comes from the word *"avon"* (עָוֹן), which is *"iniquity"* as explained in an earlier chapter. The word *avon* stands for *willfully twisting, distorting, or perverting the ways of God*.

Joshua's iniquity had the power to put a *soiled garment* over him even though he was the High Priest. Though he knew the things of God, he was also walking in a form of self-righteousness that had soiled his garment. According to the passage above, when the garments are taken away from Joshua, it is noted that his *"iniquity"* is taken away from him. The iniquity was in the garments! These filthy garments represented Joshua's guilt. Guilty of what? *Avon*; twisting, distorting, or perverting the ways of God. This is what *Avon* looks like in the realm of God: *a soiled garment*.

Those filthy garments are soiled with *sin* and *transgressions*. The Hebrew word translated as *sin* in English is *"Chata'ah"* (חַטָּאָה), which means *"missing the mark."* The English word, *transgression* is translated from the Hebrew word *"Pesha"* (פֶּשַׁע), which means to *willfully act rebellious towards God*. The person knows what they are doing is wrong, but they continue doing it anyway. "Let your garments always be white…" (Ecclesiastes 9:8) It is spiritually and physically impossible for a man or woman to wash *their own* garments.

We need God's intervention for this impossible task. Otherwise, we walk in *filthy rags* though we think they look like fine robes. "But He was wounded for our transgressions (Pesha), He was bruised for our iniquities (Avon); The chastisement for our peace was upon Him, And by His stripes we are healed." (Isaiah 53:5) God's mercy is displayed when He says, *"... See, I have removed your iniquity from you, and I will clothe you with rich robes…."* The phrase *"...rich robes..."* is translated from the Hebrew word *"machalatsah"* (מַחֲלָצָה), which denotes clothes worn for very special festive occasions, i.e., not worn every day. The only other scripture where this Hebrew word shows up is the following:

"In that day, the Lord will take away the finery; …. the festal apparel (מַחֲלָצָה)…." (Isaiah 3:18 & 22) As David says: "Blessed is he whose transgression (Pesha) is forgiven, Whose sin (Chata'ah) is covered." (Psalm 32:1) Let us seek and appreciate God's abundant mercy and let Him forgive our transgression, remove our iniquities,' and cover our sin by helping us "discard our soiled garments" and with his glorious light let Him put on us new garments that are glorious and are always white.

The Way of the Lord: fully revealed and fully manifest

Yeshua Christ came to open the way of righteousness to us so we can eat from the tree of life. Not to dwell too much on the dealings of the children of Israel because self-righteousness is an all-nation problem rooted from Adam. You become righteous only one way; God gives you the gift of righteousness, then as you now have his righteousness, you can stand before him as righteous! That *is* the *Way of the LORD!* That is the *Way of Righteousness!* That is what Abraham discovered and when he believed this, it was given to him as a gift, and he became righteous. Thus, he commanded his household to keep this revelation. Praise God!!

"For if by the one man's offense death reigned through the one, much more those who receive abundance of grace and of *the gift of righteousness* will reign in life through the *One*, Jesus Christ. Therefore, as through one man's offense judgment came to all men, resulting in condemnation, even so through one Man's righteous act the free gift came to all men, resulting in justification of life. For as by one man's disobedience many were made sinners, so also *by One Man's obedience many will be made righteous.*" (Romans 5:17-19)

This is the way of the Lord Abraham commanded his household to keep. This is what John was sent to set straight in the minds of the children of Israel before Yeshua would begin his ministry. This is the instruction that Apollos was given, which allowed him to *accurately* teach the things of God. If only his children knew his ways, the things of God would be taught accurately.

"What then shall we say that Abraham our father has found according to the flesh? For if Abraham was justified by works, he has something to boast about, but not before God. For what does the Scripture say? "Abraham believed God, and it was accounted to him for righteousness." (Romans 4:1–3)

As you can see for yourself, Abraham did nothing but only believe (*be fully persuaded by God*) and God gifted him full and total righteousness. We cannot be counted righteous in his eyes by the things we do; it is impossible.

However, once God gifts you his righteousness, good news.

1. You become righteous in his eyes,
2. It is forever, not based upon our whimsical emotions, "Your righteousness is an everlasting righteousness, And Your law is truth." (Psalm 119:142)
3. Nothing can be added to it or taken from it, "I know that whatever God does, It shall be forever. Nothing can be added to it, And nothing taken from it. God does it, that men should fear before Him." (Ecclesiastes 3:14)
4. It is irrevocable. "For the gifts and the calling of God are irrevocable." (Romans 11:29).

Praise God!

When Abraham opened his eyes to see how God *'gifted'* him righteousness, he did not plead but commanded his children and household in the *'Way of the Lord.'* To emphasize the nature of God's work, the scripture describes David having the revelation of *"imputing"* righteousness as you can see below: "Just as David also describes the blessedness of the man to whom God *imputes righteousness apart from works*: "Blessed are those whose lawless deeds are forgiven, And whose sins are covered; Blessed is the man to whom the Lord shall not impute sin." (Romans 4:6–8)

According to the Strong's Concordance, the Greek word translated as *"imputes"* is *"logízomai"* (λογίζομαι) which comes from the root of the English terms *"logic, logical"* i.e., properly, compute, *"take into account"*; reckon (come to a "bottom-line"), i.e., reason to a logical conclusion (decision). The same righteousness that was imputed to Abraham is also imputed to us.

"Now it was not written for his sake alone that it was imputed to him, but also for us. It shall be imputed to us who believe in Him who raised up Jesus our Lord from the dead, who was delivered up because of our offenses, and was raised because of our justification." (Romans 4:23–25)

Walking from Faith to Faith

For Abraham to *"...walk before Me and be blameless...,"* as the LORD required of him in *Genesis 17:1*, God had to reveal Himself to Abraham through *levels of his faith*. Learning to be aware of the levels of faith is key to walking in the way of the Lord. Faith has a law. Let us go through the levels of faith Abraham went through to walk with God.

The first level of Faith:
Believing that the LORD God is the only true God.

The first level of faith Abraham had was believing that the LORD God is the only true God. This gift of faith was passed down to Abraham through his forefather *Shem*. Shem was one of Noah's three sons and the Bible makes it was clear that, *"...from these the whole earth was populated..."* (*Genesis 9:19*) and *"...These were the families of the sons of Noah, according to their generations, in their nations; and from these the nations were divided on the earth after the flood..."* (*Genesis 10:32*). The whole earth was filled with the descendants of Noah's three sons, and they were divided into nations. We all descended from Noah's three sons. Let no one deceive you about your origins as there are multitudes of *"...doctrines of demons..."* rampant on the earth today about our origins. However, we should know that Noah had found favor in God's eyes (*Genesis 6:8*) and he was a righteous man (Hebrews 11:7). As you read in Genesis Noah became drunk one day and was naked. His son Ham saw him naked and told his brothers, Shem and Japheth who covered Noah and refused to see him naked. For this, Noah as a man of God prophesied this specifically about Shem: "Blessed be the LORD, the God of Shem, ..." (Genesis 9:26)

Noah prophesied grace into Shem that He would have revelation that The LORD is God, and He would be *the God of Shem*! Shem would pass this revelation down to his descendants. That is why it is important to note that the genealogy of Noah's three sons was all detailed in *Genesis 10* before the Tower of Babel was built. However, after the tower is built in Genesis 11 and God scatters the nations over the face of the earth, the Scriptures focus only on Shem's genealogy, where we are introduced to Abram.

This was the son whose descendants believed in the LORD as their God even after the Tower debacle. "This is the genealogy of Shem: Shem was one hundred years old ...Nahor lived twenty-nine years, and begot Terah. After he begot Terah, Nahor lived one hundred and nineteen years, and begot sons and daughters. Now Terah lived seventy years, and begot Abram, Nahor, and Haran." (Genesis 11:10, 24-26)

Therefore, by the grace given to Shem through prophecy by Noah, Abram knew through his forefather that the LORD was their God and there was no other God. How do we know Abram believed in Him alone? Because in Genesis 12, Abram does not question who the LORD is but immediately obeys Him.

"Now the Lord had said to Abram: "Get out of your country, From your family And from your father's house To a land that I will show you. I will make you a great nation; I will bless you And make your name great; And you shall be a blessing. I will bless those who bless you, And I will curse him who curses you; And in you all the families of the earth shall be blessed." So, Abram departed as the Lord had spoken to him, and Lot went with him. And Abram was seventy-five years old when he departed from Haran." (Genesis 12:1–4)

It might be obvious to you as you have read the Bible and know the story but, in those days, there was no Bible for Abram. Abram had to believe that the voice he was hearing was of God, who is the LORD. In *Genesis 14:22*, Abram makes it clear who his God is when he tells the King of Sodom, *"...I have raised my hand to the LORD, God Most High, the Possessor of Heaven and Earth, ..."* Abram did not acknowledge or give glory to any other god. He knew that the God of Shem was the *"...the LORD, God Most High, the Possessor of Heaven and Earth, ..."*

Today, Israel's greatest prayer is called *'The Shema,'* which is summarized in the following verse: "Hear, O Israel: The Lord our God, the Lord is one! (Deuteronomy 6:4)

The word *"Hear"* is translated from the Hebrew word *"Shema"* (שְׁמַע). This is a prophetic directive from a Prophet (Moses) for Israel to hear! It is not an opinion for debate: it is a command. In this one verse, the Jewish people affirm that there is only one God: The LORD our God! There are no other gods beside Him.

Interestingly, the Shema is closely followed by the following next verse: "You shall love the Lord your God with all your heart, with all your soul, and with all your strength." (Deuteronomy 6:5) It is impossible to fulfill the above commandment without understanding the Shema. Yeshua demonstrates this when he was questioned about the *"first commandment of all"*:

"Then one of the scribes came, and having heard them reasoning together, perceiving that He had answered them well, asked Him, "Which is the first commandment of all?" Jesus answered him, "The first of all the commandments is: 'Hear, O Israel, the Lord our God, the Lord is one. And you shall love the Lord your God with all your heart, with all your soul, with all your mind, and with all your strength.' This is the first commandment." (Mark 12: 28–29)

Yeshua includes the Shema as part of the *"first of all commandments."* He says, "*…This is the first commandment…*" He meant his entire answer to the question. This means you cannot love the LORD God with all your heart, soul, mind, and strength without first believing that "*…The LORD our God, the LORD is one….*"

Why? If you have many 'gods,' how can you concentrate all your heart, soul, mind, and strength on all of them? If you have forty thousand gods as I heard once on a tour when visiting an exotic place, how could you love all forty thousand of them with all your heart, soul, mind, and strength? It is impossible! So, God made it easy: He is God, and He is only one! The Shema came from Moses to establish what Abraham believed: in One God, the "*…The LORD, the God of Shem….*"

So, the Shema is a prophetic direction from Moses that was to guide the children of Israel into the level of faith Abraham walked.

The second level of faith: *Trusting What the Lord God says and living by His promises*

Since Abram believed that the LORD was God, he trusted that what the LORD God said was truth and he could trust his every Word and his promises. In Genesis 12:1, The LORD asks Abraham to leave everything and go "*…To a land that I will show you….*" Abram had to trust that the land God was going to show him later was real. He made the decision to leave all he knew, took his family with him, and went by promises made by God. That is the second level of faith-Trust! Imagine telling your immediate family to pack up all their belongings, put them in a moving van with your car being towed, and then get onto a highway without specifically putting a destination in your GPS. While driving on the highway, your nephew who happens to be the only child living with you at the time asks you where you are going, and you tell him you are moving to a place God will show you! You would have to hear from God and trust that what you heard was truth and dependable, otherwise, everyone in the van would be nervous.

Abram did just that. He did not waiver at God's promise. He trusted what God said. "He did not waver at the promise of God through unbelief, but was strengthened in faith, giving glory to God, and being fully convinced that what He had promised He was able to perform…" (Romans

4: 20–21) Now we have the recorded Words of God and do hear from his voice. Do we trust in what He says? "Today, if you will hear His voice: 8 "Do not harden your hearts, as in the rebellion," (Psalm 95:7–8) Do not waiver when you hear his voice but, be fully convinced that what He has spoken and promised, He can perform and fulfill.

The third level of faith: *Believing what God says about you.*

God let Abram know through his words what He believed about Abram. Your faith should never be about what you believe about yourself, but *what God says about you* as *"...Faith comes by hearing and hearing the word of God..."* (Romans 10:17). Abram believed what God said about him. God believed that *Abram (meaning Exalted Father)* was *Abraham (meaning Father of many nations)*. Abram was indeed a senior in age as it says in *Genesis 12:4, "...And Abraham was seventy-five years old when he departed from Haran..."* and he was without children as it says in *Genesis 15:2, "...LORD God, what will You give me, seeing I go childless..."* The LORD answered him by saying in verses 4 and 5, *"...one who will come from your own body shall be your heir...Look now toward heaven and count the stars if you are able to number them...so shall you descendants be."*

God saw Abram not only as a Father but as a Father of multitudes. And there were not just mere multitudes, but they would also be "stars" among them; meaning they will shine from the heavens, i.e., they will be *righteous* and *turn others to righteousness*. "Those who are wise shall shine Like the brightness of the firmament, And those who turn many to righteousness Like the stars forever and ever." (Daniel 12:3)

God saw Abram as Abraham, the Father of many nations, the Father of many "stars" *and Abram believed what God saw about him!* And immediately it says this: "And he believed in the LORD, and He accounted it to him as righteousness." (Genesis 15:6) Abraham believed what God said about him and God counted that as righteousness! Do you believe what God says about you? If you do, consider that righteousness. If you do not, and believe more in what the secular world says about you, consider that unrighteousness and repent. It was later in Genesis 17, that the LORD confirms this in Word, but Abram had already believed:

"When Abram was ninety-nine years old, the Lord appeared to Abram and said to him, "I am Almighty God; *walk before Me and be blameless.* And I will make My covenant between Me and you and will multiply you exceedingly." Then Abram fell on his face, and God talked with him, saying: "As for Me, behold, My covenant is with you, and you shall be a father of many nations. No longer shall your name be called *Abram, but your name shall be Abraham*; for *I have made you* a father of many nations. I will make you exceedingly fruitful; and I will make nations of you, and kings shall come from you." (Genesis 17:6)

God told Abram to be blameless. Why? Because He was already a righteous man as declared in *Genesis 15:6*. Now that you are righteous, *walk* as a righteous person: blameless! Also, notice God changes Abram's name to Abraham. It is not because that is the moment Abram becomes Abraham. God had always *"made"* Abram a father of many nations as He says, *"...for I have made you a father of many nations...."* The English word *"made"* in this verse is translated from the Hebrew phrase *"nitatika"* (נְתַתִּיךָ:), which is from the Hebrew root word *"natan"* (נָתַן), which means *"to give."* *"Nitatika"* is in the past tense as it comes from *"nitati,"* which means *"I was given."* God gifted Fatherhood upon Abram!

For seventy-five years Abram did not know God had *given him Fatherhood* until it was revealed to him as we read in Genesis fifteen. Once he heard from God and believed in the promise of the manifestation, he became ready to be a recipient of what was already given to him in heaven. God has a calendar. He knows when the manifestation of what He prepared for you will manifest.

When Abram was ninety years old, God brought the Word of his promise into Abraham's body by announcing the changing of his name from Abram to Abraham. This was not just a simple name change but a wearing of a new *Spiritual Garment* that God had kept for Abraham until that moment. For God does not do things by the flesh but by his Spirit: "... 'Not by might nor by power, but by My Spirit,' Says the Lord of hosts." (Zechariah 4:6)

For Abram had been Abraham all along but did not yet have the garment God had kept for him in heaven that would enable him to manifest and fulfill the mandate of being a *"father of many nations."* Anyone can be a father on earth but to be a "father of many nations" is different. To be one in whom, *"...all the families of the earth shall be blessed..."* is different. This was not an ordinary garment. This was a thing of the Spirit: very supernatural.

"Whatever one is, *he has been named already*, For it is known that he is man; And he cannot contend with Him who is mightier than he." (Ecclesiastes 6:10)

As it says above, Abraham was *named already*. The name you are given in heaven by God comes with a function, a garment, anointing, power, provision, authority, etc. God gives you a name before you are born. He knows you before you come out of your mother's womb. He names you with a *"... good name…,"* which you only find when you have a relationship with Him. "A good name is to be chosen rather than great riches, Loving favor rather than silver and gold." (Proverbs 22:1)

God can reveal your heavenly name or your heavenly function on the earth. A name is more powerful than a title or function. A name is more than great riches. "Listen, O coastlands, to Me, And take heed, you peoples from afar! The Lord has called Me from the womb; From the matrix of My mother, He has made mention of My name." (Isaiah 49:1)

The Prophet Isaiah says God called him from the womb. He states God made mention of his name from the womb of his mother. Abraham was named Abraham before he was born. It takes hearing from God to know your heavenly name, which has your full potential in it. It is God's announcement that makes you aware of your name in Heaven.

As God named you *already*, it is important to find out what He named you, believe in what He calls you, and wait for the transfer of the substance of it on his calendar. It is believed in the Jewish community that a name change can affect a person's identity and destiny. They have the phrase, *"meshaneh shem, meshaneh mazal,"* which means *"a change of the name causes a change in fate."* God also changed Sarai's name to Sarah:

"Then God said to Abraham, "As for Sarai your wife, you shall not call her name Sarai, but *Sarah shall be her name*. And I will bless her and also give you a son by her; then I will bless her, and she shall be a mother of nations; kings of peoples shall be from her." (Genesis 17:15–16)

The name Sarah means Princess. In God's eyes, she is Royalty. Please understand that God honored the names they had previously. The Book of Exodus is called *"Shemot"* in Hebrew, which means *"names."* It begins with God naming the descendants of the Fathers, Abraham, Isaac, and Jacob. He names them individually because He knows them by name and loves them. However, at times God may have to change one's destiny by changing their name to the one He ordained for them. This is what happened with Abram and Sarai. Later we see this with Jacob:

"So, He said to him, "What is your name?" He said, "Jacob." And He said, "Your name shall no longer be called Jacob, but Israel; for you have struggled with God and with men and have prevailed." (Genesis 32:27–28)

The name *"Israel"* (יִשְׂרָאֵל) means *"Prince with God."* Recall Sarah was called a Princess? She gave birth to Royalty with Isaac! Isaac's children were Royalty. We see Moses changing Hoshea's name to Joshua before spying out the land: "These are the names of the men whom Moses sent to spy out the land. *And Moses called Hoshea the son of Nun, Joshua."* (Number 13:16)

"Hoshea" (הוֹשֵׁעַ) means *"to Save"* or *"to Rescue"* and Joshua, which is translated from *"Yehoshua"* (יְהוֹשׁוּעַ) means *"The LORD is Salvation."* Moses, a Prophet made the name change. A Prophet hears from God. This name change was significant in that it gave Joshua the Spiritual strength and understanding that no matter how big the giants were in the land, the LORD would be Israel's Salvation in taking the land.

Yeshua also changed Simon, the son of Jonah's name to Peter, "Jesus answered and said to him, "Blessed are you, Simon Bar-Jonah, for flesh and blood has not revealed this to you, but My Father who is in heaven. And I also say to you that *you are Peter*, and on this Rock I will build My church, and the gates of Hades shall not prevail against it." (Matthew 16:17–18)

The name *"Peter"* is translated from the Greek word *"Petros"* (Πέτρος), which means *"a stone (pebble)."* Yeshua meant Simon was a *"living stone"* since the father had revealed this revelation to him. Simon was the first of the living stones that would be laid on top of *"The Rock"* (Christ) to build God's congregation. Peter also understands this as he writes: "…you also, as living stones, are being built up a spiritual house, a holy priesthood, to offer up spiritual sacrifices acceptable to God through Jesus Christ." (1 Peter 2:5)

Peter was not *the* "Rock" on which the church is built. Christ has always been the Rock. "all ate the same spiritual food, and all drank the same spiritual drink. For they drank of that spiritual Rock that followed them, and *that Rock was Christ."*(1 Corinthians 10:4)

There are more examples of name changes in the Bible. Just a side note: a popular myth is that Yeshua also changed Saul's name to Paul. He did not. Saul who was Jewish was also called *"Paulos"* (Παῦλος), which is a *Latin* name he used in his interactions with the Romans who were ruling the Land of Israel in his day: "*Then Saul, who also is called Paul*, filled with the Holy Spirit, looked intently at him" (Acts 13:9)

The main point here is that they believed in what God called them. They believed what God said about them when He changed their names. You must believe what God says about you. "For the earnest expectation of the creation eagerly waits for the revealing of the sons of God." (Romans 8:19)

How will the sons of God be revealed before God announcing it? God knows the day of their manifestation. Do you believe you are a son of God? That is what it says about his children in the above verse. If so, are you hearing his voice as Abram did? Are you waiting patiently, never wavering but believing the promise until the day of your announcement? Do not become sluggish!

"And we desire that each one of you show the same diligence to the full assurance of hope until the end, that you do not become sluggish, but imitate those who through faith and patience inherit the promises." (Hebrews 6:11–12)

The fourth level of faith: Believing God has made you Righteous

Abraham did not *reckon* himself as righteous until God reckoned Abraham as righteous. God is the One Who declared Abraham righteous. This is the key to walking on the way of the Lord: Abraham believed what God believed about him! Abraham believed he was righteous because God said Abraham was righteous.

When you believe what God believes about you, that He has made you righteous, you will walk in the way of the LORD's thoughts about you. The LORD thinks you are righteous, so be what He thinks about you already. When you walk in the way of the LORD, you walk as a friend because friends think alike. That is why it says,

"And the Scripture was fulfilled which says, "Abraham believed God, and it was accounted to him for righteousness." And he was called *the friend of God*." (James 2:23) Abraham believed in God in everything. Never did he question what God said to him. Did he have questions? Absolutely! Did he get answers? Yes!

"But you, Israel, are My servant, Jacob whom I have chosen, The descendants of Abraham My friend." (Isaiah 41:8) A friend is one you can reveal everything you hold dear, and they will believe in you, support you, understand you, etc. Abraham was like this with God. Abraham believed in God being good! He believed every word God spoke to him. So, God could walk with him and share things with him. It is from faith to faith that Abraham, the righteous man walked. And he continued in more levels of faith, greater than I could summarize. Abraham went from *"…faith to faith…"* believing he was righteousness.

"For with the heart one believes unto righteousness, and with the mouth, confession is made unto salvation." (Romans 10:10) It was *"from faith to faith" that Righteousness was revealed* to Abraham. Just as the Gospel reveals the same to us. "For I am not ashamed of the gospel of Christ, for it is the power of God to salvation for everyone who believes, for the Jew first and also for the Greek. For in it the righteousness of God is revealed from faith to faith; as it is written, "The just shall live by faith." (Romans 1:16–17)

As Abraham did, so are we to live from faith to faith. The phrase, "The just shall live by faith" comes from this verse in the prophets: "Behold the proud, His soul is not upright in him; But the just shall live by his faith." (Habakkuk 2:4) The word *"just"* is translated from the Hebrew word *"tsaddiq"* (צַדִּיק), which means "Righteous" as we have discussed before. So, this verse could be read as follows: "Behold the proud, His soul is not upright in him; But the Righteous shall live by his faith." (Habakkuk 2:4)

Faith in what? Faith in getting things from God? Faith in operating in the gifts of God? Faith in God? Yes, those and more but primarily, a righteous person shall live by faith in his/her righteousness that has been supplied by God. Since the righteousness of God has been revealed to you, *have faith that you are righteous*! Live by this faith first!! Why? Because the Righteous in God's eyes have *many benefits* like the verses below on prayer as an example: "The Lord is far from the wicked, But *He hears the prayer of the righteous.*" (Proverbs 15:29)

God hears the prayers of a righteous person, and this has results: "The effective, fervent *prayer of a righteous man* avails much." (James 5:16) The prayer of a righteous man avails much because God hears it and answers him. There are many more benefits for the righteous listed in the Bible. So, the key to walking in the way of the Lord is to have faith that you are Righteous! You are righteous because God has made you righteous! *So, the righteous person should live by this faith: that he/she is righteous in the eyes of God!*

A disclaimer must be added: because you are righteous, God commands you like He commanded Abraham: "I am Almighty God; walk before Me and *be blameless.*" (Genesis 17:1)

As they say, do not just talk the talk, walk the walk! Walk before God as a righteous person who is blameless! This is possible with the Grace of God through the Holy Spirit as it says: "For *the grace of God* that brings salvation has appeared to all men, *teaching us* that, denying ungodliness and worldly lusts, we should live soberly, righteously, and godly in the present age," (Titus 2:11–12)

The *grace of God teaches you to deny* ungodliness and worldly lusts. By this, if you are listening, He is teaching you to live *soberly, righteously,* and *godly* in the present age: *be blameless!*

Chapter 7

The Prophet Like Moses

The Prophet from the Region of the Galilee

"The Lord has chastened me severely, But He has not given me over to death. Open to me the gates of righteousness; I will go through them, And I will praise the Lord. *This is the gate of the Lord*, through which the righteous shall enter. I will praise You, For You have answered me, And have become *my salvation. The stone which the builders rejected Has become the chief cornerstone.* This was the Lord's doing; It is marvelous in our eyes. This is the day the Lord has made; We will rejoice and be glad in it." (Psalm 118:18–24)

The "...*Gate of the Lord through which the righteous shall enter* is this: "...the *Stone which the builders rejected*...." The phrase "*the builders*" is translated from the Hebrew word "*habonim*" (הַבּוֹנִים), which comes from the Hebrew root "*banah*" (בָּנָה), from where you get the Hebrew word "*banim*" (בָּנִים), which means "*sons.*" So, in Hebrew thought, the '*builders* can also mean '*sons.*' This can be demonstrated with the following verse: "So, Sarai said to Abram, "See now, the Lord has restrained me from bearing children. Please, go in to my maid; perhaps I shall obtain children by her." And Abram heeded the voice of Sarai." (Genesis 16:2)

The phrase "...*shall obtain children*..." is translated from the Hebrew word "*ebane*" (אִבָּנֶה), which means "*I will be built*" yet the English includes the word "...*children*..." because the Hebrew root does indicate *children as builders*. So, the builders who are children or sons rejected the Stone, which

God picked as the Chief Cornerstone! who are the children? "He came to His own, and His own did not receive Him." (John 1:11)

In the phrase *"...and His own...,"* the *"own"* here is from the Greek word *"idios"* (ἴδιος), which means, *"one's own people."* His own people did not receive Him. Now, I want to make this clear, I love the Jewish people and I am not making it a point to have any case against them for not receiving Him. There is a lot of anti-Semitism in the church because of misunderstanding of Scripture. He was not received because of this one Truth: "...A prophet is not without honor except in his own country and in his own house." (Matthew 13:57)

Most prophets are celebrated after they are gone. We read about and celebrate the prophets mentioned in the Bible but when they were alive, they were not honored as much as we think. Some were even killed.

"Then He said, "Assuredly, I say to you, no prophet is accepted in his own country. But I tell you truly, many widows were in Israel in the days of Elijah, when the heaven was shut up three years and six months, and there was a great famine throughout all the land; but to none of them was Elijah sent except to Zarephath, in the region of Sidon, to a woman who was a widow. And many lepers were in Israel in the time of Elisha the prophet, and none of them was cleansed except Naaman the Syrian." (Luke 4:24–27)

Though we read with amazement about Elijah's and Elisha's exploits, it says there were *"...many widows..."* in Elijah's day, but God only sent him *"...to Zarephath...who was a widow."* And though there were *"...many lepers..."* in Elisha's days, he only cleansed one, *"...Naaman the Syrian...."* Why? Out of the many widows and lepers in Israel, only Zaraphath and Naaman *honored* or *accepted* Elijah and Elisha as prophets at that time. The word *"accepted"* in the above verse is from the Greek Word, *"dektos"* (δεκτός), which is an adjective derived from the Greek Word, *"dexomai"* (δέχομαι), which means *"...receive in a welcoming way...."* "*He who receives a prophet* in the name of a prophet shall receive a prophet's reward..." (Matthew 10:41)

Zarephath and Naaman received the Prophet's reward because they received and honored Prophet Elijah and Prophet Elisha, respectively. So, one of the signs that Yeshua is the *Mashiach* is that He was not *"...received by his own...."* Am I implying He was a Prophet? Yes! Moses did tell the children of Israel about the *Mashiach* coming as a Prophet: "The Lord your God will raise up for you a Prophet *like me* from your midst, *from your brethren*. Him you shall hear, according to all you desired of the Lord your

The Prophet Like Moses

God in Horeb in the day of the assembly, saying, 'Let me not hear again the voice of the Lord my God, nor let me see this great fire anymore, lest I die.' "And the Lord said to me: 'What they have spoken is good. I will raise up for them a *Prophet like you from among their brethren*, and will put My words in His mouth, and He shall speak to them all that I command Him." (Deuteronomy 18:15–18)

God said this Prophet would come "*...from among their brethren....*" This Prophet would be from among Israelite brethren. He did not say from any other nation. This Prophet would be Jewish! Also here is the catch: Moses said, "*...a Prophet like me....*" God also confirmed to Moses that this Prophet would be "*...a Prophet like you from among their brethren....*" Not only was this Prophet going to be like Moses, but He was also going to be Jewish. There are multiple great prophets in the Bible, but Moses was unique in two areas:

"Then the Lord came down in the pillar of cloud and stood in the door of the tabernacle and called Aaron and Miriam. And they both went forward. Then He said, "Hear now My words: If there is a prophet among you, I, the Lord, make Myself known to him in a vision; I speak to him in a dream. Not so with My servant Moses; He is faithful in all My house. *I speak with him face to face,* Even plainly, and not in dark sayings; And *he sees the form of the Lord*. Why then were you not afraid To speak against My servant Moses?" (Numbers 12:5–8)

This Prophet also must speak with God, "*...face to face....*" To be a Prophet like Moses was going to be a huge feat, as it says: "But since then, there has not arisen in Israel a prophet like Moses whom the LORD *knew face to face*, in all signs and wonders which the Lord sent him to do in the land of Egypt, before Pharaoh, before all his servants, and in all his land, and by all that mighty power and all the great terror which Moses performed in the sight of all Israel." (Deuteronomy 34:10–12)

The Israelites understood that a Prophet would rise among them that would do signs and wonders in a manner not seen since Moses' time. Yeshua is recorded as having done mighty signs and wonders more spectacular than those done by anyone since Moses and many saw this as the sign of Him being *the* Prophet:

"Therefore, many from the crowd, when they heard this saying, said, "Truly this is *the* Prophet." Others said, "This is the Christ." But some said, "Will the Christ come out of Galilee? Has not the Scripture said that the Christ comes from the seed of David and from the town of Bethlehem, where David was?" So, there was a division among the people because of Him." (John 7:40–43)

The New Testament already records that He was born in Bethlehem in the lineage of King David. However, there was division among the people because they did not expect the *Mashiach* to *"...come out of the Galilee..."* Even the chief priests and Pharisees had this argument:

"They answered and said to him, "Are you also from Galilee? Search and look, *for no prophet has arisen out of Galilee.*" (John 7:52) Why was the *region of Galilee* a contention? Because Solomon had given it to Hiram. "Now it happened at the end of twenty years, when Solomon had built the two houses, the house of the Lord and the king's house (Hiram the king of Tyre had supplied Solomon with cedar and cypress and gold, as much as he desired), that King Solomon then gave Hiram twenty cities *in the land of Galilee.*" (1 Kings 9:10–11)

It was a place for gentiles: "... By the way of the sea, beyond the Jordan, In Galilee of the Gentiles...." (Isaiah 9:1) It is recorded how Yeshua ended up in the region of Galilee: "But when he heard that Archelaus was reigning over Judea instead of his father Herod, he was afraid to go there. And being warned by God in a dream, he turned aside *into the region of Galilee.* And he came and dwelt in a city called Nazareth, that it might be fulfilled which was spoken by the prophets, "He shall be called a Nazarene." (Matthew 2:22–23)

Though they knew a lot of what the prophets had said about the *Mashiach*, they had missed this one by Isaiah: "Nevertheless the gloom will not be upon her who is distressed, As when at first He lightly esteemed. The land of Zebulun and the land of Naphtali, And afterward more heavily oppressed her, By the way of the sea, beyond the Jordan, In *Galilee of the Gentiles.* The people who walked in darkness *Have seen a great light;* Those who dwelt in the land of the shadow of death, *Upon them a light has shined."* (Isaiah 9:1–2)

So, they say, *"...Search and look, for no prophet has arisen out of Galilee."* They did not search and look hard enough in the Scriptures to see what Isaiah wrote about the Light dawning in the Galilee. The region of Galilee was despised, especially Nazareth: "And Nathanael said to him, "Can anything good come out of Nazareth?" ..." (John 1:46)

Interestingly, the Hebrew Gospel of Matthew states, "...הנביא נאזרת יקרא...," which reads as follows in the English, *"Prophet Nazareth he will be named" Isaiah* said it was a place where *"...people walked in darkness..."* and also known as the *"...land of the shadow of death...."* However, this is the region God chose. "Surely the Lord God *does nothing Unless* He reveals His secret to His servants the prophets." (Amos 3:7)

He revealed the secret to the prophet Isaiah that the *Mashiach* would come from the region of the Galilee. If the chief priests and pharisees of that day were more discerning of God's secrets revealed by the prophets, the despised region of the Galilee would be the first place to look! God can choose the most rejected people and despised places to bring forth his purpose. David who was the youngest was picked rather than his handsome elder seven brothers (*1 Samuel 16:6-13*). God chose Gideon as a mighty leader for Israel though he was from the weakest tribe, and he was the least in his family (*Judges 6:11-16*). It is this very reason that God chose the nation of Israel from all the nations of the earth: "The LORD did not set His love on you nor choose you because you were more in number than any other people, *for you were the least of all peoples;*" (Deuteronomy 7:7)

It was for this reason that God chose to hide and plant the *Mashiach* in the region of Galilee, a place with the greatest need in Israel. Wouldn't you begin a major rescue in the most affected area of a disaster? It was during the darkest region in Israel and the most affected by the *shadow of death* that God chose to begin the dawning of his Light. God showed Isaiah that is where He was going to start. The people walking in darkness would see, *"...a great light..."* and those who dwelt in this land of the shadow of death, *"...upon them a light has shined...."* The *Mashiach* is the Light that they would see; the Light that would shine upon them. This is recorded in the New Testament:

"Now when Jesus heard that John had been put in prison, *He departed to Galilee.* And leaving Nazareth, He came and dwelt in Capernaum, which is by the sea, in the regions of Zebulun and Naphtali, *that it might be fulfilled which was spoken by Isaiah the prophet,* saying: "The land of Zebulun and the land of Naphtali ... By the way of the sea, beyond the Jordan, Galilee of the Gentiles: The people who sat in darkness have seen a great light, And upon those who sat in the region and shadow of death Light has dawned." (Matthew 4:12-13, 15-16)

From that time Yeshua began to preach and to say, "Repent, for the kingdom of heaven is at hand."

If this was not the *Mashiach* in the Galilee, then my question is *when* is the Light going to dawn for those in the Galilee as Isaiah prophesied? To this day there have not been any Jewish or Christian writings documenting anything significant coming out of that region apart from the story of Yeshua! As the region was called that *"...of the gentiles...,"* no wonder gentiles have been fascinated by the Light that started in this small place. Our Jewish brothers must understand that the Light fascinates the gentiles that dawned from the region of the Galilee.

"And in that day *there shall be a Root of Jesse*, Who shall stand as a banner to the people; For *the Gentiles shall seek Him, And His resting place shall be glorious."* (Isaiah 11:10)

There have been and there are still many great Jewish Rabbis, great Jewish religious scholars, and well-known Jewish *Tzadikim* or *'righteous people.'* However, Isaiah says of the one called, *"...a Root of Jesse..."* that, *"...the Gentiles shall seek Him...."* Isn't any Jewish brother or sister curious as to why the Gentiles have not sought any of them as much as the Jewish man called Yeshua? There is no man more famous than Yeshua as far as the Gentiles are concerned!

Even those who do not believe in Him have heard of Him. Tourists go to *Galilee* from all over the world to see where Yeshua came from. Otherwise, what does Nazareth have to offer that attracts so many global visitors? It is from this previously despised place that God raised the Prophet the Jewish people are still waiting for.

No Gentiles could make up such an elaborate *Jewish* story! It is not a conspiracy. The Gentile nations had no idea about any *'Mashiach'* as they did not have *Holy Prophets* pointing to Him in their cultures. One thing the gentiles understand by the mercy of God is the Light when they see it, as they were previously in darkness. When the Light shines, they come to it: "Arise, shine; For your light has come! And the glory of the Lord is risen upon you. For behold, the darkness shall cover the earth, And deep darkness the people; But the Lord will arise over you, And His glory will be seen upon you. *The Gentiles shall come to your light*, And kings to the brightness of your rising." (Isaiah 60:1-3)

The Light is a Jewish Messiah who brings Salvation: "Indeed, He says, 'It is too small a thing that You should be My Servant To raise up the tribes of Jacob, And to restore the preserved ones of Israel; I will also give *You as a light to the Gentiles*, That *You should be My salvation* to the ends of the earth.'" (Isaiah 49:6)

No Name has brought the Gentiles more towards the *"...God of the Hebrews..."* than the Name of Yeshua. It is through Him that the Gentile *Christians* have for the most part (not entirely) gotten rid of the lies of their fathers i.e., idolatry: "O Lord, my strength, and my fortress, My refuge in the day of affliction, The Gentiles shall come to You From the ends of the earth and say, "Surely *our fathers have inherited lies, Worthlessness and unprofitable things. Will a man make gods for himself, Which are not gods?"* (Jeremiah 16:19–20)

About that Prophet from the Galilee, Moses said, "...*Him you shall hear...*" (*Deuteronomy 18:15*)

"Now it came to pass, about eight days after these sayings, that He took Peter, John, and James and went up on the mountain to pray. As He prayed, the appearance of His face was altered, and His robe became white and glistening. And behold, two men talked with Him, who were Moses and Elijah, who appeared in glory and spoke of His decease which He was about to accomplish at Jerusalem. But Peter and those with him were heavy with sleep; and when they were fully awake, they saw His glory and the two men who stood with Him. Then it happened, as they were parting from Him, that Peter said to Jesus, "Master, it is good for us to be here; and let us make three tabernacles: one for You, one for Moses, and one for Elijah"— not knowing what he said."

"While he was saying this, a cloud came and overshadowed them; and they were fearful as they entered the cloud. And a voice came out of the cloud, saying, "This is My beloved Son. *Hear Him!*" When the voice had ceased, Yeshua was found alone." (Luke 9:28–36)

Moses and Elijah were witnesses to confirm that not only is this *the* Prophet, *but He is also the Son of God! Hear Him!*

The Zohar, The Star, and the Scepter

"Those who are wise shall shine Like the *brightness* (Zohar) of the firmament, And those *who turn many to righteousness Like the stars* forever and ever." (Daniel 12:3)

In the above verse, the English term *"brightness"* is from the Hebrew word *"Zohar"* (זֹהַר), which can be translated as *"shining"* and is only found in one other verse: "Then I looked, and there was a likeness, like the appearance of fire—from the appearance of His waist and downward, fire; and from His waist and upward, like the appearance of brightness (Zohar), like the color of amber." (Ezekiel 8:2)

Those who turn many to righteousness will *"Zohar"* or *shine* like the Stars forever. But I want you to know the above verse from Daniel 12 says "*...those who turn many to righteousness...*" This means if the Earth is here, there are *"those"* who are turning many to righteousness! As you recall, Abraham was guarding the *Way of Righteousness* as he had commanded his household. This explains why God told Abraham this about his descendants:

"And behold, the word of the Lord came to him, saying, "This one shall not be your heir, but one who will come from your own body shall be your heir." Then He brought him outside and said, "Look now toward heaven, and *count the stars* if you are able to number them." And He said to him, "*So shall your descendants be.*" And he believed in the Lord, and *He accounted it to him for righteousness.*" (Genesis 15:4-6)

God gave Abraham a revelation: his descendants shall be like *the stars*, meaning out of his descendants there will be *"those"* that turn many to righteousness! The belief in God's word that the heir coming out of his body will bring descendants who are like the stars was accounted to Abraham as *righteousness*!! Your descendants cannot be righteous if the Father is not righteous!

The revelation that he will have an heir from his body *and* that his descendants will be stars is what he believed for God to account righteousness to Abraham! Now does that mean "all" Abraham's descendants will cause many to be righteous? No! Other descendants will be concerned only with earthly things and may not be involved in turning many into righteousness, that is why God also says this: "Also your descendants shall be as the dust of the earth; you shall spread abroad to the west and the east, to the north and the south; and in you and in your seed all the families of the earth shall be blessed." (Genesis 28:14)

There will be those like *"stars"* who will turn many to righteousness and those *"as the dust"* who will not be concerned about turning anyone to righteousness but will be only concerned about earthly things! God called the entire nation of Israel to be a light to the nations. However, as an entire nation will have stars or dust, God had to use the phrase, "*...in you and in your seed...*" to point out how "*...all the families of the earth shall be blessed....*"

Such a "Star" was spoken of that would turn many to righteousness as noted in the book of Numbers "*...A Star shall come out of Jacob; A Scepter shall rise out of Israel,...*" (Numbers 24:17) So, this Star is also a Scepter! And this Star shall come out of Jacob: this Scepter shall rise out of Israel.

Where in Israel is this Scepter coming from? "The *Scepter shall not depart from Judah*, Nor a lawgiver from between his feet," (Genesis 49:10)

So, this Scepter is from the Tribe of Judah! From whom in the tribe of Judah? Though there are other scriptures, the one below because of the word *"Bethlehemite"* as the Scepter was going to end up in Bethlehem: "...I am sending you to Jesse the Bethlehemite. For I have provided Myself a king among his sons." (1 Samuel 16:1) "...He raised up for them David as king, to whom also He gave testimony and said, 'I have found David the son of Jesse, a man after My own heart, who will do all My will.' From this man's seed, according to the promise, God raised up for Israel a Savior—Jesus" (Acts 13:22–23)

How do we know He was a the *"Star"* that would come out of Jacob to turn many to righteousness? The sign itself of a Star showed up at the time of his birth:

"Now after Jesus was *born in Bethlehem of Judea* in the days of Herod the king, behold, wise men from the East came to Jerusalem, saying, "Where is He who has been born *King of the Jews*? For *we have seen His star* in the East and have come to worship Him." ... When they heard the king, they departed; and behold, *the star* which they had seen in the East went before them, till it came and *stood over where the young Child was. When they saw the star,* they rejoiced with exceedingly great joy." (Matthew 2:1–2; 9–10)

The Wise men themselves confirmed He was born "...*King of the Jews*..." With every King comes a Scepter and as we had read before, "A *Scepter shall arise out of Israel*..." So, what type of Scepter is He carrying? "But to the Son He says: "Your throne, O God, is forever and ever; A *scepter of righteousness* is the scepter of Your kingdom." (Hebrews 1:8; Psalm 45:6)

The Scepter of the Kingdom is a Scepter of *Righteousness*! If it is a scepter of righteousness, then it is used to "execute" righteousness. Therefore, righteousness should be a result! So, how can we confirm that this 'One' star executed righteousness? The Bible confirms this: "For as by one man's disobedience many were made sinners, so also by *One Man's* obedience *many will be made righteous.*" (Romans 5:19)

Chapter 8

A Gift From Heaven

Righteousness Looks Down from Heaven

Righteousness is received from Heaven. That is why Yeshua says the following: "Nevertheless I tell you the truth. *It is to your advantage that I go away*; for if I do not go away, the Helper will not come to you; but if I depart, I will send Him to you. And when He has come, He will convict the world of sin, and *of righteousness*, and of judgment: of sin, because they do not believe in Me; *of righteousness, because I go to My Father and you see Me no more*; of judgment, because the ruler of this world is judged. "I still have many things to say to you, but you cannot bear them now. However, when He, the *Spirit of Truth,* has come, He will guide you into all truth" (John 16:7–13)

Why does Yeshua say, *"…of Righteousness because I go to My Father, and you see Me no more…"?* The explanation is given by the following verse: "Mercy and truth have met together; Righteousness and peace have kissed. *Truth shall spring out of the earth*, And righteousness shall look down from heaven." (Psalm 85:10–11)

The phrase *"look down"* is translated from the Hebrew word, *"nishkaf"* (נִשְׁקָף), which means *"to be seen"* or *"to be viewed."* So, righteousness is *seen* or *viewed from Heaven.* Interestingly, the Hebrew root of the word *'nishkaf'* is *"shakef"* (שָׁקַף), which means *"reflected."* Our righteousness should reflect the one in Heaven! The reason Yeshua had to go up to Heaven is that *"… Righteousness shall look down from heaven.…"* Why? *He had to go up so that He can send us the gift of Righteousness from Heaven!* As John explained:

"A man can receive nothing *unless it has been given to him from heaven.*" (John 3:27) Yeshua had to ascend so that He can give us gifts *"from heaven."* As it says: *"When He ascended on high, He led captivity captive, And gave gifts to men."* (Ephesians 4:8) He had to go up and send the Holy Spirit, the *"Spirit of Truth"* down to us to *"...guide you into all truth..."* because Truth remains on the earth, as it says, *"...Truth shall spring out of the earth...."* Why does Truth remain on the earth? Because the word truth in the above verse can be translated from the Greek word *"alétheia"* (ἀλήθεια), which means *"Reality."*

So as *Righteousness comes from heaven, we walk in reality (truth) on earth when our Righteousness is from Heaven.* Jesus says He is *"...the Way, the Truth (alétheia -Reality) and the Life..."* (John 14:6). He is the *reality,* not the *illusion* given by the world. His righteousness is from Heaven, not the illusion of righteousness given to us by men. We are to reflect the righteousness given from Heaven. The Spirit of Truth was sent to guide us *"into all"* His reality!

Since we have established that Yeshua had to ascend so that he could send us his gift of righteousness, it says the following in Romans 10: "But the righteousness of faith speaks in this way, "Do not say in your heart, *'Who will ascend into heaven?'" (that is, to bring Christ down from above)"* (Romans 10:6) If we bring Him down, then He cannot send gifts from heaven. "Or '"who will descend into the abyss?'" (that is, to bring Christ up from the dead)." (Romans 10:7) He already ascended as He is alive, so, it would be useless to even try to descend to get Him. However, the verse continues:

"But what does it say? "The word is near you, in your mouth and in your heart" (that is, the word of faith which we preach): that if you confess with your mouth the Lord Jesus and believe in your heart that God has *raised Him from the dead,* you will be saved." (Romans 10:8–9)

The Holy Spirit who has come down from Heaven brings the word *"near you,"* He puts it *"in your mouth and in your heart."* Only one who is alive can save you and one Who is ascended can save all on the earth as opposed to saving a few in one physical location. In addition, only God can send the Holy Spirit!! So, if Yeshua sends down the Holy Spirit, *He is LORD!* This alone should make you *"...confess with your mouth the Lord Yeshua..."*

If He is ascended, it is obvious He was raised from the dead! That is something you have no option but to believe if you agree that He is ascended and He sent the Holy Spirit from above. So, because righteousness *looks down from heaven* and you have believed in your heart that *"God raised Him from the dead,"* because He is already ascended to Heaven, this is what you receive: "For with *the heart one believes unto Righteousness,* and *with the mouth confession is made unto salvation."* (Romans 10:10)

This is the most astounding thing in the Scripture! A righteousness that comes down from Heaven straight into your heart just by believing that *One Who* has ascended is God and He has sent you the gift from above!! This is not a righteousness resulting from what you do, or you do not do: it is a *Righteousness of Faith*. That is why it says:

"For the Scripture says, "*Whoever believes on Him will not be put to shame*. For there is no distinction between Jew and Greek, for the same Lord over all is rich to all who call upon Him. For "*whoever calls on the name of the Lord shall be saved*." (Romans 10:11–13)

To conclude, this is the way of righteousness: "For Christ is *the end of the law for righteousness* to everyone who believes." (Romans 10:4)

Imputed Sin

It is interesting when God warned Adam and Eve about eating from the tree of the knowledge of good and evil, He only mentioned that they will *surely die*. He did not mention sin. Eating from the tree would bring death to them and the world. "And the Lord God commanded the man, saying, "Of every tree of the garden you may freely eat; but of the tree of the knowledge of good and evil you shall not eat, for in the day that you eat of it *you shall surely die*." (Genesis 2:16–17)

What God meant was instead of Adam reigning, *death would reign over him* and that would eventually cause Adam and his offspring to die. When death reigns, life is cut off. The serpent knew they needed an *opening* to bring death into the world and that conduit was *sin*. The first time the word '*sin*' shows up in the Bible is when God explains to Cain his condition: "So the Lord said to Cain, "Why are you angry? And why has your countenance fallen? If you do well, will you not be accepted? And if you do not do well, *sin lies at the door*. And *its desire* is for you, but *you should rule over it*." (Genesis 4:6–7)

God says to Cain sin was waiting at the *"door"* to come in. The English word *"door"* in this passage is translated from the Hebrew word *"Pethach"* (פֶּתַח), which is translated as an *"opening," "doorway"* or *"entrance."* The *"entrance"* for Adam and Eve for *"sin"* was their *"eyes."* "Then the serpent said to the woman, "You will not surely die. For God knows that in the day you eat of it *your eyes will be opened*, and you will be like God, knowing good and evil." (Genesis 3:4–5) Their eyes were an *"entrance"* for sin, while their mouth was the entrance for death to enter. The serpent wanted them to open both. As you can see below:

"So, when the woman saw that the tree was good for food, that it was pleasant to the eyes, and a tree desirable to make one wise, she took of its fruit and ate. She also gave to her husband with her, and he ate. Then the eyes of both of them were opened, and they knew that they were naked; and they sewed fig leaves together and made themselves coverings." (Genesis 3:6–7)

By eating the fruit, the *entrance* of their eyes was opened, allowing sin to enter, which brought death with it. Interestingly, the word *"eye"* in Hebrew is *"ayin"* (עַיִן). In the above verses, the phrase *"your eyes"* is translated from the Hebrew word *'eineichem'* (עֵינֵיכֶם). The Hebrew root for the word "ayin" (eye) is where the word *'ma'ayan'* (מַעְיָן) comes from, which means *'spring'* or *'water source.'* So, to go deeper, you could say through the opening of their eyes they became *a spring or water source of good and evil.* "A righteous man who falters before the wicked Is like a murky spring (ma'ayan) and a polluted well." (Proverbs 25:26)

Recall, earlier I explained that the function of the name Adam could be noted as a *"strong or leading door for the waters, blood or chaos"* coming from God, as God was Adam's source. When their eyes were opened, their waters became polluted with sin and death, and they became a *'water source'* from which the whole of humanity sprung from. We came out of a murky spring.

The well from which we sprung (born) was polluted. Adam's water and blood were polluted, and this pollution was automatically translated to Eve. Then from Eve's womb, we were all born. *"Does a spring send forth fresh water and bitter from the same opening?"* (James 3:11) In this case, the *"same opening"* or womb did spring forth fresh and bitter water. As you may already know from science, amniotic fluid begins with water from the mother's body. From Eve's womb, we were *all born* out of her water.

That is why Yeshua said we must be born of water through baptism or immersion. "Nicodemus said to Him, "How can a man be born when he is old? Can he enter a second time into *his mother's womb and be born?"* Jesus answered, "Most assuredly, I say to you, *unless one is born of water and the Spirit, he cannot enter the kingdom of God."* (John 3:4–5)

The concept of immersion in water was not new as we have discussed. The *Mikvah* or water immersion for purification is to this day important part of Jewish life as seen in verses like *Leviticus 22:6–7* and *Leviticus 15:16*. In Hebrew culture, it is understood that a *Mikvah* is a *womb from where a rebirth happens.* By Yeshua letting us know we must be born of water, He was saying we must be "rebirthed" out of a different womb or different waters.

As you can see above, Nicodemus asked Him, "*...Can he enter a second time into his mother's womb and be born?*" Nicodemus understood Yeshua was talking about *rebirth*. He just did not know how it would happen. Then Yeshua explained, we must be rebirthed from above, born in new waters, and born from the womb of the Spirit of God. This needed to happen for anyone to "*...enter the Kingdom of God....*" So, the immersion or baptism of John was not a baptism for a *'membership in a congregation'* as I have heard at times. It was for a *rebirth in new waters.*

"And he went into all the region around the Jordan, preaching a baptism of repentance for the remission of sins," (Luke 3:3) As we discussed earlier, the Hebrew word for repentance is Teshuva, which means to do a complete turnaround and return to God. So, the baptism of John was for a person to '*...return to God and be rebirthed in His waters...*' So as one was immersed or baptized in the baptism of John, they would descend into the water in death and enter the *new womb* full of *new waters* and ascend as 'reborn.'

The immersion would cut one off from the waters of Eve, which were contaminated with sin and death that is why it is a baptism for the "*...remission of sins....*" The English word *"remission"* is translated from the Greek word *"aphesis"* (ἄφεσις), which means "*...dismissal, release, pardon...*" or *forgiveness.* The same word is used in the following verse: "For this is My blood of the new covenant, which is shed for many for the remission of sins." (Matthew 26:28) Therefore, it says the following after Moses: "Nevertheless death reigned from Adam to Moses, ..."(Romans 5:14) "But where sin abounded, grace abounded much more, so that as sin reigned in death," (Romans 5:20–21)

It says sin was *reigning in death* and death reigned but when Moses came, death's reign ceased. Why? Moses was able to remove the sin of Israel so that death could not reign anymore. Outside of the Levitical sacrifices, Moses gave the entire nation of Israel a water baptism: "Moreover, brethren, I do not want you to be unaware that all our fathers were under the cloud, all passed through the sea, all were baptized into Moses in the cloud and in the sea," (1 Corinthians 10:1–2)

A Gift From Heaven

The passing through the sea was a baptism for the nation of Israel. The baptism of John was from heaven: "But He answered and said to them, "I also will ask you one thing, and answer Me: The baptism of John—was it from heaven or from men?" And they reasoned among themselves, saying, "If we say, 'From heaven,' He will say, 'Why then did you not believe him?'" (Luke 20:3–5)

After the rebirth in water is done, then there would have to be a rebirth in the Spirit. That is why it says, *"...our fathers were under the cloud...."* Why is the baptism of the Spirit necessary? Because the Spirit is the source of everything concerning life. *John 6:63*, says, *"...It is the Spirit Who gives life...."* God's intention was for us to also become *sources of life* with rivers of living waters coming out from within us.

That is why Yeshua had to give us different water. "Jesus answered and said to her, "Whoever drinks of this water will thirst again, but whoever drinks of the water that I shall give him will never thirst. But the water that I shall give him will become in him a fountain of water springing up into everlasting life." (John 4:13–14)

"On the last day, that great day of the feast, Jesus stood and cried out, saying, "If anyone thirsts, let him come to Me and drink. He who believes in Me, as the Scripture has said, out of his heart will flow rivers of living water." But this He spoke concerning the Spirit, whom those believing in Him would receive; for the Holy Spirit was not yet given, because Jesus was not yet glorified." (John 7:37–39)

We see the progression from the water baptism to the Spirit baptism: "And it happened, while Apollos was at Corinth, that Paul, having passed through the upper regions, came to Ephesus. And finding some disciples he said to them, "Did you receive the Holy Spirit when you believed?" So, they said to him, "We have not so much as heard whether there is a Holy Spirit." And he said to them, "Into what then were you baptized?" So, they said, "Into John's baptism." Then Paul said, "John indeed baptized with a baptism of repentance, saying to the people that they should believe on Him who would come after him, that is, on Christ Jesus When they heard this, they were baptized in the name of the Lord Yeshua. And when Paul had laid hands on them, the Holy Spirit came upon them, and they spoke with tongues and prophesied." (Acts 19:1–6)

God had a better plan than the first one. So, what is sin? Strong's translates the English word sin in Genesis 4:7 from the Hebrew word, *"Chatta'ah"* (חַטָאָה). This is from the Hebrew root word *"Chet"* (חֵטְא), which means to *"miss the mark"* as a sharpshooter missing his or her target (bullseye) when shooting a gun.

So, what happened to humanity through Adam is described in Romans as follows: "Therefore, just as *through one man sin entered the world, and death through sin, and thus death spread to all men, because all sinned*" (Romans 5:12) Because he *missed the mark*, we who came out of him *all missed the mark* as well. Through Adam's *mistake*, sin entered the world and death used sin as the vehicle to enter in.

"Nevertheless, death reigned from Adam to Moses, even over those who had not sinned according to the likeness of the transgression of Adam, who is a type of Him who was to come." (Romans 5:14)

Death was ruling over all even those who had not sinned though sin was also in the world. However, there was a drastic change with sin when Moses brought *the law*. "For until the law sin was in the world, but sin is not imputed when there is no law. (Romans 5:13)

Before Moses, sin could not be imputed! That is why God did not mention sin to Adam but only death. However, with the law of Moses, every sin began to be *imputed*! To clarify, the English word *"impute"* in the above verse was translated from the Hebrew word *"Chashab"* (חָשַׁב). Chashab means *"to think"* or *"account."* It also means to *"compute"* or *"reckon."* As discussed earlier, Strong's notes the root of this word means to *"plait or interpenetrate"* or to literally *"weave"* or generally *"fabricate."*

Therefore, with the law of Moses, when one sinned, the sin was *"accounted,"* or they were reckoned as *"sinners"* as the sin was now *"woven"* in them and had become part of them! This is significant as it now was not just an action but had become woven within the person! Recall what God told Cain: "If you do well, will you not be accepted? And if you do not do well, *sin lies at the door. And its desire* is for you, but *you should rule over it.*" (Genesis 4:7)

God told Cain regarding sin that he *"should rule over it."* From Adam to Moses, man could rule over sin. However, once sin was imputed through the law, it *"reigned"* in man. "Moreover, *the law entered that the offense might abound. But where sin abounded, grace abounded much more, so that as sin reigned in death,* even so, grace might reign through righteousness to eternal life through Jesus Christ our Lord." (Romans 5:20–21)

Death was reigning over man before Moses. When Moses introduced the law, Adam's offense abounded, and sin was now *imputed*, therefore "*sin reigned in death.*" So now not only was death reigning over man but also sin was reigning in death! To be more precise, death was reigning *over* all men while sin reigned *within* man.

"Therefore, do not let sin reign in your mortal body, that you should obey it in its lusts." (Romans 6:12) As sin was now reigning in man's mortal bodies, it had *dominion* over man because of the law. "For *sin shall not have dominion over you,* for *you are not under law* but under *grace.*" (Roman 6:14) Apart from the law, sin did not have any dominion. However, sin got an opportunity under the law through the commandment.

"What shall we say then? Is the law sin? Certainly not! On the contrary, *I would not have known sin except through the law*. For I would not have known covetousness unless the law had said, "You shall not covet." *But sin, taking opportunity by the commandment*, produced in me all manner of evil desire. *For apart from the law sin was dead.* I was alive once without the law, but when the commandment came, sin revived, and I died." (Romans 7:7–9)

Imputed Righteousness: The Joy of Forgiveness

"Blessed is he whose transgression is forgiven, Whose sin is covered. Blessed is the man to whom the Lord does not *impute* iniquity, And in whose spirit, there is *no deceit*." (Psalm 32:1–2)

Most Jews and Christians celebrate the concept of their transgression being forgiven and their sin being covered, as the Bible makes clear above. However, few know or consider verse two which makes it clear that a man is *"blessed"* to whom the LORD *does not impute* iniquity! So, it is no longer just forgiving a man's sins daily or once a year, but there is a level where God *does not impute a man's iniquity*! That is mind-blowing!

The English word *"impute"* in the above verse was translated from the Hebrew word *"Chashab"* (חָשַׁב). Chashab means *"to think"* or *"account."* It means to *"compute"* or *"reckon."* As discussed earlier, Strong's notes the root of this word means to *"plait or interpenetrate"* or to literally *"weave"* or generally *"fabricate."* So, if God chooses not to impute iniquity to a man, there must be something He interpenetrates! He instead imputes righteousness.

A Deeper Understanding of Righteousness (Tzedakah)

The Hebrew word *"Tzedek"* (צֶדֶק) means Justice, i.e., bringing *"equity."* This word comes from three Hebrew letters, (צ - ד - ק). These *"root"* letters give you the *"tree"* the root will produce and the branches and fruits. This is just my way of explaining how the Hebrew language builds from root letters. I would say the branches and fruits are produced when extra letters are added to the three Hebrew root letters. When the letter Hey (ה) is added at the end of the word Tzedek, you get the word *"Tzedakah"* (צְדָקָה), as shown in the passage below about Abraham:

"And he believed in the LORD, and He accounted it to him for *righteousness* (צְדָקָה)." (Genesis 15:6) The roots and stems of the tree *of God* are Justice, with righteousness as *the trunk* and *branches* and the *fruits* of Life coming out of the branches. "…that they may be called *trees of righteousness*, The planting of the LORD, that He may be glorified." (Isaiah 61:3)

That is why the Messiah was prophesied as a *"branch"* as in the following: "There shall come forth *a Rod* from *the stem* of Jesse, And *a Branch* shall grow out of *his roots*…" (Isaiah 11:1) Notice the words Rod, stem, and roots in the above verse. "Behold, the days are coming, "says the LORD, "That is I will raise to David a *Branch of Righteousness*; A King shall reign and prosper…" (Jeremiah 23:5)

And the people: "Also, your people shall all be *righteous*; They shall inherit the land forever, *The Branch* of My planting, The works of My hands, That is I may glorified." (Isaiah 60:21) Though we can go deeper about the *Tree of God* (Compare Jeremiah 11:16 and Romans 11:16–27), I want to highlight the word *"Tzedakah"*, which is also translated as *"Charity"* in Jewish tradition.

This is significant because if you think about a tree, when it produces fruit, it is very generous. The fruit is produced whether you the recipient of the fruit is good or bad, lazy, or diligent, tall, or short, etc. The tree gives freely. Indeed, you can say God created a fruit tree to give *out of generosity*. Let me explain. Once a fruit tree starts to produce fruit, it will continue producing fruit in season until the tree dies. It is the easiest way to feed humankind (non-commercially). Otherwise, most herbs must be worked in their season to produce a harvest after challenging work.

The birds, animals, or fish that we consume do not make it easy. There is work involved in catching birds, fish, and animals for food. But a fruit tree does not run or hide its fruit from you. It does not evade you like animals when you want to eat its fruit. You do not have to wear fatigues and sit quietly in the bush hiding before you shoot an arrow for fruit like when trying to get deer meat.

A Gift From Heaven

A fruit tree generously displays its fruit for you to eat and drops them when they are rotten to produce even more for you. If fruit trees had been as evasive as animals, I think humans would have missed an abundance of edible, essential food. Interestingly, the fruit tree was created only for man as you can see below. Only herbs were for the birds, animals, and everything that creeps on the earth.

"And God said, "See, *I have given you every herb* that yields seed which is on the face of all the earth, and *every tree whose fruit yields seed*; to you it shall be for food. Also, to every beast of the earth, to every bird of the air, and to everything that creeps on the earth, in which there is life, I have given every green herb for food;" and it was so." (Genesis 1:29–30)

This changed after the flood of Noah's time. My point is because Righteous also means "charity" or generosity, it is the conduit through which God delivers his blessing on the earth. That is why it says God "credited" Abraham's account with "righteousness." Abraham was not only a recipient of God's "charity," but God made Abraham, himself *a* Charity. That is why it says Abraham would "...*be a blessing*..." and through Abraham, "...*all the families of the earth shall be blessed*...." We all have accounts in heaven where righteousness is credited. This righteousness not only benefits us as we become filled with righteousness but also that we can become like God and be a *"blesser"* to others.

To be righteous does not mean a person who walks around with a collar around his neck or seems docile to the world, but it means a person endued with God's supernatural charity. That is why we have scripture like the following: "I have shown you in every way, by laboring like this, that you must support the weak. And remember the words of the Lord Jesus that He said, '*It is more blessed to give than to receive*.'" (Acts 20:35)

"Jesus said to him, "*If you want to be perfect*, go, sell what you have and *give to the poor*, and *you will have treasure in heaven*; and come, follow Me." (Matthew 19:21)

"Give, and it will be given to you: good measure, pressed down, shaken together, and running over will be put into your bosom. For with the same measure that you use, it will be measured back to you." (Luke 6:38)

The money you have or earned, which you give to someone or an organization that did not work for it at all.

The word Tzedak incorporates what the following Hebrew letters stand for:

Gimmel (ג)	those who give from "Gomel"	*to bestow*
Dalet (ד)	dal	*impoverished*
Hay (ה)	full potential	
Gimmel, Dalet, Hey		*to bestow upon the impoverished so that they come to their full potential.*

We come into our true potential when we give. The *Hey* is the full potential of the person who has received from a giver. That is why the *Hey* comes at the end of the word Tzedakah.

God distributes wealth so that the wealth is distributed around the world. The wealthy are God's servants who distribute the wealth. When you give to others, it opens the door from heaven to give you much more than you gave.

"Speak to the children of Israel, that they bring Me an offering. From everyone who gives it willingly with his heart, you shall take My offering." (Exodus 25:2) The phrase, "*...bring Me an offering...*" actually reads like this in Hebrew, "*...Take me a donation....*" (...תְּרוּמָה לִי וְיִקְחוּ...). What did He mean, *"take"* instead of giving? You end up taking so much more than you give to the donation. God said the result would be that He would live '*within*' them. That is the result was much more than what they gave!

Notice God says, "*...everyone who gives it willingly with his heart....*" They were to collect only from those who were generous. It adds, "*...you shall take My offering....*" This would be received from those who generously donated while attaching it to God, specifically in their hearts. Otherwise, a donation can be for anything. But this donation had to be one that the giver would give specifically to God, therefore the phrase, "*...My offering....*"

It is with these types of donations that in the Book of Malachi (3:10), God says "*...Try me now in this....*" The Recipient in this case (God) gives so much more to the bestower than the bestower gives to God. God is naturally a Bestower. When He asks for a gift to be given to Him, He is intending for that gift to be placed in his Name. His Name automatically blesses whatever it touches and then He returns it to the bestower as a gift from Him. The bestower becomes a recipient with a much larger and more expanded gift.

Now the recipient has the potential to be a bigger bestower towards God and when he gives, God returns an even larger gift. And the *cycle of abundance* goes on and on. Abram gave a TENTH to God (Genesis

14:19–20). Abraham was not only a recipient of God's generosity, but God made Abraham a bestower of blessings. That is why it says Abram would *"...be a blessing..."* and through Abram, *"...all the families of the earth shall be blessed...."* (Genesis 12:3). God began this by *crediting* Abraham's account with righteousness (Genesis 15:6). The purpose of *'abundance'* is righteousness. The way of the Lord is the Way of righteousness. This righteousness comes from God.

In the Book of John, Yeshua does say that *He* is the *way!* "Jesus said to him, "*I am the Way, the Truth*, and *the Life*. No one comes to the Father except through Me." (John 14:6) If Yeshua is the way, how did Abraham *'command'* his household to *'keep'* the way of the Lord? Abraham's household did not know Yeshua. However, Abraham had been blessed with a glimpse of Yeshua in his time as confirmed by Yeshua Himself below.

"Your father Abraham rejoiced to see My day, and *he saw it* and was glad." (John 8:56) Like Abraham, let us rejoice to see Yeshua's day (*light*) and be those who through faith in him are gifted righteousness! Let us live by this Faith: *We are righteous, and it is all God's doing!*

About the Author

Duncan Katende Ndugwa is a Prophetic Teacher who was radically transformed by the Lord through an encounter in 2006 and was given, by grace, an abundance of the Spirit of Revelation to edify the Body of Christ. By 2008, he was an Associate Pastor in a multi-cultural church and was also a member of a Messianic Jewish congregation in Omaha, Nebraska. He has led multiple Bible study groups, revival meetings and ministered in several churches in Nebraska, Iowa, and Kansas. Duncan continues to minister with Prophetic insight and revelation.

For more information and about his latest audio or video messages, connect with Duncan through these social media channels and receive revelational teachings that bring glory to the Lord:

Facebook.com/Prophet Duncan Katende
Youtube.com/Prophet Duncan Katende
Instagram: @Duncan Katende

Bibliography

Cambridge Dictionary. "aspects." In Cambridge Dictionary.org. https://dictionary.cambridge.org/us/dictionary/english/aspect.

Howard, George. *Hebrew Gospel of Matthew*. Georgia: Mercer University Press, 1995

Luzzatto, Moshe Chaim. *The Way of God and Ma'armar halkkarim. An Essay on Fundamentals*. Translated and annotated by Aryeh Kaplan. Jerusalem: Feldheim, 1998.

M. Rosenbaum and A.M. Silbermann. *Pentateuch with Rashi's commentary, 1929-1934*. https://www.sefaria.org/Rashi_on_Genesis.14.13.2?lang=bi&with=all&lang2=ennnections

Onkelos and Jonathan Ben Uzziel. *The Targums of Onkelos and Jonathan Ben Uzziel On The Pentateuch*. Translated by J.W. Etheridge. London. Longman, Green, Longman, and Roberts, 1862.

Talmudic Israel/Babylon. "*Bereishit Rabbah*." Sefaria Community Translation. https://www.sefaria.org/Bereishit_Rabbah.68.2?lang=bi&with=About&lang2=en

The American Heritage Dictionary of the English Language. "Fabricate." In The American Heritage dictionary.com. https://www.ahdictionary.com/word/search.html?q=fabricate

The American Heritage Dictionary of the English Language. "Interpenetrate." In The American Heritage dictionary.com. https://www.ahdictionary.com/word/search.html?q=Interpenetrate

The American Heritage Dictionary of the English Language. "Plait." In The American Heritage dictionary.com. https://www.ahdictionary.com/word/search.html?q=Plait

The American Heritage Dictionary of the English Language. "Weave." In The American Heritage dictionary.com. https://www.ahdictionary.com/word/search.html?q=weave

Tosafot. *Daat Zkenim*. Translated by Rabbi Eliyahu Munk. https://www.sefaria.org/Daat_Zkenim_on_Genesis.12.3.1?lang=bi&with=About&lang2=en

CPSIA information can be obtained
at www.ICGtesting.com
Printed in the USA
BVHW031407021222
653305BV00014B/675